The Great Mystery of the Second Coming

The Great Mystery of the Second Coming

THE GOSPEL OF THE GLORY OF CHRIST

Gail Anne Carroll O.F.S

ISBN: 1537316508
ISBN 13: 9781537316505

Dedication

To Father Mary Joachim Tierney, O.C.S.O., who nurtured in the author a deep love for Saint Paul and a longing to come to know the mystery of Christ's Second Coming hidden in his epistles and now being unveiled.

Of this astounding unveiling of Sacred Scripture Father Joachim in his booklet <u>The Second Coming</u> has written, "Blessed are they who hear *'The Gospel of the Glory of Christ;'*[1] that is to say, 'the Mystery of the Second Coming' when it is preached by the Church. They will share in Mary's Immaculacy." Sharing in Mary's Immaculacy can be equated to living in the Kingdom of God's Divine Will on earth – as due the angels and saints in Heaven.

---

1 2 Corinthians 4:4

Table of Contents

CHAPTER 2

THE RISE OF GOD'S KINGDOM INTO WHOLENESS

CHAPTER 3

THE NUMBER THREE AND THE DIVINE RISING

CHAPTER 4

GOD THE FATHER: INVISIBLE – SPIRIT – WATER

CHAPTER 5

GOD THE SON: VISIBLE – SOUL – SALT

CHAPTER 6

<u>YEAST - THE LEAVEN OF THE PHARISEES</u>
112

CHAPTER 7

THE GOSPEL OF THE GLORY OF CHRIST

CHAPTER 8

THE BASILICA DOMES OF
ST. LAWRENCE AND ST. PETER

CHAPTER 9

- THE HOLY SPIRIT -
THE CROWNING OF JESUS' ANOINTED BODY
RISEN AND GLORIFIED.

CHAPTER 10

THE OLIVE TREE
LADY WISDOM
THE WOMAN OF THE REVELATION

CHAPTER 11

THE MARRIAGE COVENANT IS BOUND THROUGH:

CHAPTER 12

THE GREAT CONSUMMATION OF CHRIST'S MARRIAGE TO HIS CHURCH

ADDENDUM
206

Preface

It was a beautiful spring morning in the Blue Ridge Mountains of Western North Carolina. I had stepped outside to take in a breath of fresh air. Lulled by an unusual quiet, a calm peacefulness overshadowed me as I slowly scanned the landscape of evergreen and budding trees, over which stood distant mountain views. Raising my heart to God in gratitude for the beauty before me, I gazed upward to see brilliant sunlight dominating the vibrant blue sky. Although there was no threat of rain, several cumulous clouds billowed overhead. Enveloped in the grace that dwells in the present moment my eyes fixed on a particularly luminous cloud. Unknowingly, I had entered the eternal realm where time and space do not exist. My faculties suspended, I was drawn into the wondrous splendor of God's creation when I heard a strong celestial voice declare "The Glory of God appeared in a cloud."

With an unprecedented feeling of peace my senses were reactivated. Still beholding the cloud, my mind inquisitively began to probe. "Is it possible that God's Glory is reflected in the elements of a pure cloud—water and salt? This might explain why Father Joachim persists in putting blessed and exorcised salt in the Holy

Water[2] he blesses, despite the fact that its use by the Church has become optional."

I then recalled how another devout priest, my pastor, had recently encouraged me to take home some of the Holy Water he had just blessed. To which I intuitively responded, "Why, Father, are you now putting the blessed and exorcised salt in the water?" He emphatically replied "Yes, the other blessing was not effective against the demons—they flee from this!"

Next, I was given over to ponder the significance of the Cloud of God's Glory as it relates to the water and salt[3] used in the sacrament of Baptism—the very sacrament through which we enter into God's Kingdom of Glory.

Turning to Sacred Scripture, not only was my speculation confirmed that God uses the natural elements of water and salt to represent His supernatural Glory, in Exodus 16:10 I came across the very words I had heard the celestial voice announce *"The glory of God appeared in a cloud."* This affirmed that something very powerful was being presented to me. Yet three years would pass before the astounding knowledge of the elements of water and salt—illuminating God's plan to restore His Kingdom of Glory on earth—would begin to unfold in a most profound way.

It was in the early afternoon of March 17, 1999, and the Abbot and Prior of Our Lady of the Holy Spirit Monastery, in Conyers, Georgia, were knocking at my door. They had driven over four hours to discuss and confirm their plan for one of the monastery's

---

2 Not only did Father Joachim faithfully use the traditional water and salt blessing, he fervently made hundreds of copies of it which he placed next to his altar by the gallons of this Holy Water he made available to all. Not surprisingly, people came from far and near for this powerful sacramental.

3 Although the traditional use of blessed and exorcised salt in the waters of Baptism has in recent time become optional.

Founding Fathers, Father Mary Joachim Tierney, O.C.S.O., to be cared for by me in the last days of his earthly life. This was taking place, in part, because the monastery had been struck with an epidemic of pneumonia. Father Joachim, whose lungs were already compromised, had succumbed to it. With labored breathing he had been taken to the hospital where he had been admitted, had gone into respiratory distress and had been put on a ventilator. At 86 years old his prognosis was poor.

Once in my home Abbot Bernard explained, "Never before has the monastery sent a monk outside the walls to die." Prior Mark stressed: "No one is to know Father Joachim is here—or when he dies." He continued: "The monastery could not contain the people who would come from around the world. For this reason, we've decided not to publicize Father's death until after his funeral." They also made a passing comment, of a dubious nature, about a woman who had been assisting Father Joachim with revelations of Jesus Christ he had received. I stood before them expressionless.

Father Joachim, my spiritual director, had nurtured in me the same deep love he had for St. Paul, as well as a fervent longing to come to know the mystery of the visions and revelations of the Lord that St. Paul was given when he was taken into the third Heaven—our future paradise—as seen in 2 Corinthians 12:1-7. What Father Joachim and I discovered was that St. Paul was shown the Mystery of Christ's Second Coming in Glory. And that the preaching of the revelation of this mystery is "St. Paul's Gospel"—now being unveiled—of which he writes: *"Now to him that is able to establish you, according to 'my gospel', and the preaching of Jesus Christ, according to 'the revelation of the mystery', which was kept secret from eternity, which 'now' is made manifest by the scriptures of the prophets…"* (Romans 16:25-26)

What was taking place was all so surreal. After all, what were the chances that the person the Abbot and Prior seemed intent on keeping Father Joachim away from, was the very person standing before them with whom they were making arrangements for him to spend his last days on earth? They had even gone so far as to drive out of state, to the secluded home of a Registered Nurse, to ensure this. This is not meant to cast a shadow on these good servants of God. They were indeed cooperating with God's Divine Will because it was not yet time for the full meaning and understanding of the revelations of Jesus Christ that were shown to St. Paul to be revealed to us.

What was even more astonishing is that Father Joachim had prophesied three years before that his mission would begin in my home. In retrospect, I believe it was this prophetic word that opened the door to the knowledge of God's Glory, mystically represented by salt and water, I had begun to receive. It is no coincidence that Father Joachim often mentioned that his mission had to do with the restoration of God's Kingdom of Glory—the New Jerusalem—to earth. It is also no coincidence that Israel's eternal inheritance is dependent on salt, after all, *"Did you not know that the Lord God of Israel gave to David the Kingdom over Israel forever, to him and to his sons by a Covenant of Salt?"* (2 Paralipomenon 13:5; 2 Chronicles 13:5)

Father Joachim came to my home and suffered tremendously, all with an enormous love and zeal to save souls, mildly complained only once, remained lucid, and was nursed back to health by the health care system, a small group of others, and myself. Then as God would have it, he returned home to the monastery—where seven days later he would enter into eternal life on May 21, 1999.

Father Joachim was a lover. He had the gift of making everyone he met feel as though he was the most special person in the world. This charism came easily because he believed it. He absolutely treasured what he often referred to as the infinite value of each and every soul. The word "no" did not exist in his vocabulary. With a twinkle in his eyes and a countenance exuding joy, he thrived ministering to an army of souls, never appearing to tire. After just two visits with him, Anne Marie Hancock in her book *Wake Up America!* describes him as "the personification of love." And indeed he was.

Ever since his passing, countless signs and wonders continue to confirm the Great Mystery of Christ's Second Coming revealed in these pages and now being launched from my home as was foretold by Father Joachim. This awesome gift of knowledge is the great enlightening grace Father Joachim said was needed to bring the New Era of Peace and Light into the world, of which he wrote, "How does one escape the defilement of the world? One of the gravest effects of the sin of Adam and Eve is the spiritual blindness of which we are all subjected. The great grace we need is the enlightenment and 'the full knowledge of the Lord and Savior Jesus Christ.' This comes only with the unfolding of the mystery of the Epiphany when *"The Gospel of the Glory of the blessed God"*[4] is made known and proclaimed."

---

4 1 Timothy 1:

Introduction

THE ASTONISHING UNVEILINGS OF SACRED Scripture in "The Great Mystery of the Second Coming" are now being revealed to prepare us—the Bride of Christ—to enter into the deepest intimacy we can possibly have with our Bridegroom Jesus, the Consummation of our Marriage.

This momentous gift of knowledge first unveils the amazing mystery contained in the Sacred Name Jesus Christ and its inversion Christ Jesus. In Chapter I we see that throughout the Gospels of Matthew, Mark, Luke, and John the life and teachings of Our Lord and Savior Jesus Christ are proclaimed—and yet not once in these Gospels is the Sacred Name Christ Jesus mentioned.

Whereas, throughout the more mysterious epistles and with particular emphasis in St. Paul's letters, the Sacred Name Christ Jesus is found—often even alternating the names Jesus Christ and Christ Jesus in the same verse![5] The Revelation of this Mystery which has been kept secret until *"now"*—what St. Paul also refers to as *"due time"*—will prove to be the preaching of Jesus Christ according to St. Paul's gospel. In his own words, *"Now to him that is able to establish*

---

5 As exampled in 1Timothy 1:1: *Paul, an apostle of Jesus Christ, according to the commandment of God our Savior and of Christ Jesus our hope;* and also I Corinthians 1:2: *To the church of God that is at Corinth, to them that are sanctified in Christ Jesus, called to be saints, with all that invoke the name of our Lord Jesus Christ, in every place of theirs and ours.*

you according to 'my gospel,' and 'the preaching of Jesus Christ,' according to 'the revelation of the mystery' kept secret [hidden] from all eternity, which 'now' is made manifest by the scriptures of the prophets..." (Romans 16:25)

Moving on to Chapter II, which metaphorically mirrors Chapter I, here we expound on the parable Jesus tells about the Kingdom of Heaven and its rise into wholeness, as seen in Matthew 13:33. This intriguing parable is about three measures of meal, to be equated to three measures of bread dough, in which a woman has hidden the rising ingredient. The secret rising ingredient, per the parable, is only to be revealed when the women's meal, to be equated to the Kingdom of Heaven, has risen into wholeness. Incredibly, after 2000 years, the woman is "now" revealing the hidden leavening ingredient. This of course indicates that the meal she is preparing—the Kingdom of Heaven—is about to rise into wholeness!

The woman who is preparing the three measures of meal proves to be none other than the Immaculate Virgin Mary, our Blessed Mother. The three basic ingredients she is using to unite her meal of bread dough are water, salt, and olive oil – as seen in Chapter III. It is no coincidence that these same three ingredients are the very three elements through which we mystically enter into the Kingdom of Heaven in the sacrament of Baptism.

The full knowledge of the Son of God's life-giving water, sanctifying salt and unction of olive oil, is so vital in preparing us to enter into the Great Mystery of the Second Coming, that Chapters IV, V and IX are devoted to covering these elements which God uses to represent and anticipate His Glory. Through this immense infusion of heightened enlightenment, it will be inexcusable for anyone to deny God's power and divinity within His people and in our midst—for the invisible things of God are clearly shown using the visible. St. Paul puts it this way: "*For the invisible things of Him, from the creation of the world, are clearly seen, being understood by the things that are made; His eternal power also, and divinity: so that they are inexcusable."* (Romans 1:20)

In Chapters VII and VIII we delve deeper into the Revelation of the Great Mystery of the Second Coming. Here again we are being prepared for entering into perfection because nothing impure can unite with God. At this point we are called to fathom the all-encompassing unity that exists in Christ's anointed and risen Body of Glory, in which, per scripture, the fullness of all things in Heaven and earth dwells. Also revealed here is the powerful significance of the last name under which God has revealed Himself to us.

God is now giving us this extraordinary, comprehensive and transforming knowledge of Himself because to grow in knowledge of Him is to grow more deeply in love with Him—and how He longs for us to know and love Him ever so intimately with our whole body, spirit and soul.

Through this unveiling of the Great Mystery of the Second Coming, Our Lord is beckoning us to enter into complete and perfect oneness with Him. A oneness wherein we shall come to see, taste and feel the immeasurable breadth, length, height and depth of His Love. Of this most edifying knowledge of God being revealed, St. Paul writes, *"For the perfecting of the saints, for the work of the ministry, for the edifying of the body of Christ; Until we all meet into the unity of faith, and of the knowledge⁶ of the Son of God, unto a perfect man, unto the measure of the age of the fullness of Christ."* (Ephesians 4:12-13)

The knowledge is the grace and the grace is the knowledge!

---

6 Father Joachim believed we needed this full knowledge of Our Lord and Savior Jesus Christ to free us from the corruption of this world. Hugh Owen in his exceptional book, New and Divine - The Holiness of the Third Christian Millennium, quotes this same verse from Ephesians 4:11-13 and then writes, "The Body of Christ comes to the sanctification of full stature by being perfected in unity. This passage seems to suggest a growth in future knowledge of Jesus that unifies the Body of Faith." Pg 13

The woman who is preparing our Marriage Feast—the three measures of meal—is elaborated on in Chapter X: She, our Blessed Mother, is also assisting in the adornment of our wedding garment, assuring it is of the finest of linen, glittering and white. This chapter promises to leave the reader with a lasting impression of awe and wonder for the woman—The Virgin of the Revelation—the pertinent title under which our Blessed Mother appeared in Three Fountains, Rome, on April 12, 1947. It is believed that the knowledge imparted in this chapter will play a decisive role in proclaiming our Blessed Mother, the Immaculate Virgin Mary, Co-redemptrix, Mediatrix of all Graces and Advocate.

Next, in Chapters XI and XII, we see how the Marriage Covenant in the natural/visible realm is a pre-figuration of our upcoming Mystical Marriage to Christ in the supernatural/invisible realm. This includes the Sacred Act of our Consummation because it too will involve: a total abandonment to our Spouse; a rising; a penetration that unveils a sacred womb; a shedding of virgin blood, which simultaneously involves a climactic outpouring of Christ's Glory; and finally, as God would have it, the conception of new life—our glorified new life in Christ! (Chapter XI beautifully complements the wisdom imparted in Saint John Paul II's talks on the Theology of the Body.)

Then, because our most noble, gallant, and majestic Bridegroom cannot be outdone in generosity, the honeymoon He has planned for His Bride (the Church/God's people) is the glorious one thousand year period of peace seen in the book of Revelation 20:4—"*...and they lived and reigned with Christ for a thousand years.*" (As the Church has always rightly taught, Our Lord and Savior Jesus Christ will not reign physically on earth during this period—the mystery of this reign of Christ is revealed herein.) In this wonderful period of peace, joy, light, and love, we will not only "be doing" God's Divine

Will on earth, but we will come to "live in" God's Divine Will, as did Adam and Eve before the fall. Ah...the ineffable splendor of God's Glory!

It is believed that this powerful explosion of grace—the full knowledge of the Son of God contained in this unveiling of The Great Mystery of the Second Coming, will not only help to heal the Great Schism of 1054, but will also be the remedy that unites in faith both our Jewish and Protestant brethren. This unity of faith takes place in the One, Holy, Catholic and Apostolic Church, and brings about what St. Paul, in the passage previously quoted, calls *"the 'measure' of the age of the fullness of Christ."*

The measure of the age of the fullness of Christ will prove to correspond to the three measures of meal the woman[7] is now unveiling. She is now revealing this knowledge because her meal, the Kingdom of Heaven, is about to rise into fullness!

---

7 Father Joachim explains here the means the Woman is now using: "Mary often expresses her presence to and in all of Her children." As in this case in which the Immaculate Virgin Mary is using this author (weak and unworthy) to express Her thoughts.

CHAPTER 1

.

§

"Now to him that is able to establish you,
according to my gospel,
and the preaching of Jesus Christ,
according to the revelation of the mystery
which was kept secret from eternity."

ROMANS 16:25

"The Revelation of the Mystery"
(Romans 16:25)

The Unveiling

We begin with a brief introduction to the meaningful words mystery, revelation and gospel and how they correspond to one another in St. Paul's gospel.

Throughout St. Paul's epistles he writes about <u>a hidden knowledge</u> which he refers to as "a mystery" or "the mystery." For example, in his letter to the Colossians 1:26 St. Paul writes: *"The mystery which hath been hidden from ages and generations but now is manifested to the saints."* The word mystery can be found as often as eighteen times in St. Paul's letters—whereas out of all four of the Gospels of Matthew, Mark, Luke and John the word mystery only appears once.

Next, there's the word "revelation" which in Sacred Scripture implies and <u>unveiling</u>. Therefore, when St. Paul writes about *"the revelation of the mystery"* he is referring to "an unveiling of hidden knowledge." The word revelation can be found as many as eight times in St. Paul's letters, however, like the word mystery, it is only found once in all four of the Gospels of Matthew, Mark, Luke and John. The one other place the word revelation is seen is in the Book of Apocalypse—also known as the Book of Revelation.

The other word relevant to this amazing unveiling of hidden knowledge is "gospel"—<u>the preaching of the revelation of Jesus Christ</u>. The word gospel can be seen as often as sixty-four times in St. Paul's epistles while only ten times in the Gospels.

St. Paul's Gospel: The fact that the words mystery, revelation, and gospel are found remarkably more often in St. Paul's writings than anywhere else in the Bible, not only indicates that they would somehow correspond to one another, but also that they would have a special connection with St. Paul. This is attested to in St. Paul's letter to the Romans 16:25-26 in which he writes: *"Now to him that is able to establish you, according to **my gospel**, and **the preaching of Jesus Christ**, according to **the revelation of the mystery** which was kept secret from eternity… which now is made manifest by the scriptures…"* Here St Paul is not only making the important point that his *gospel* is unique, but also that his *preaching of Jesus Christ* has to do with a *revelation of the mystery*—an unveiling of hidden knowledge!

St. Paul maintains that his gospel is distinct from that of the other apostles when in Galatians 1:11-12 he writes: *"For I give you to understand, brethren, that **the gospel which was preached by me is not according to man**. For neither did I receive it of man, nor did I learn it; **but by the revelation of Jesus Christ**."* Here again we see St. Paul linking his gospel to a revelation—an unveiling—of Jesus Christ!

Brethren, this unveiling of Jesus Christ that St. Paul tells us <u>he did not receive nor learn from man</u>, is the preaching of Jesus Christ according to the hidden knowledge of Jesus Christ he was given and which, as he states, is only *"now"* being manifested by the scriptures to the saints.

What makes the preaching of Jesus Christ according to St. Paul's gospel even more fascinating is that the mystery intrinsic to his gospel, *the revelation of the mystery of* Christ he was given, was revealed to him when he was taken into the future. This is evidenced in 2 Corinthians 12:1-8 where St. Paul writes that he received his *"revelations of the Lord"* (vs. 1), while *"caught up to the third heaven"* (vs. 2), where he was *"caught up into paradise,*[8] *and heard secret words..."*(vs. 4)

Wisdom be Attentive: Since St. Paul received his revelations of the Lord in the Third Heaven[9]—our future paradise—this confirms that the preaching of Jesus Christ according to St. Paul's gospel is from an entirely different perspective than the preaching of Jesus Christ according to the Gospels of Matthew, Mark, Luke and John. <u>In fact, since St. Paul's gospel was given to him in paradise to come, his preaching of Jesus Christ is from the perspective of a time when all things have already been restored to wholeness and holiness.</u>

Another verse that validates the distinctiveness of St. Paul's gospel follows: *"I wonder that you are so soon removed from him that called you into the grace of Christ, unto another gospel. Which is not another, only there are some that trouble you, and would pervert the gospel of Christ."* [10] Note how St. Paul wants us to understand that his gospel **is** and **is not** another gospel. St. Paul uses this mysterious language because his gospel—the hidden knowledge of Jesus Christ he was given in the future—was not to be revealed and preached until now.

---

8 Here we see that St. Paul identifies the Third Heaven with paradise. Keeping in mind the Church's teaching that paradise will be restored ("Oh Happy Fault!). This indicates that we can assume that the Third Heaven St. Paul was caught up into is our future paradise restored.

9 In 2 Peter 3:5-7, St. Peter instructs us that the first heaven and earth perished in water, and the second Heaven and earth which are now, are reserved unto fire against the day of judgment and the perdition of ungodly men.

10 Galatians 1:6-7

So when we consider that St. Paul was taken into the future and given a secret knowledge of Jesus Christ that is only now[11] being manifested to the saints, this tells us that his letters are in a more specific way addressed to us, which explains the following riddle he wrote to the Corinthians:

> *"But God, who is faithful, for our preaching which was to you, was not,* **It is***, and* **It is not***. For the Son of God, Jesus Christ who was preached among you by us, by me, and Sylvanus, and Timothy, was not,* **It is** *and* **It is not***, but,* **It is***, was in him. For all the promises of God are in Him,* **It is***: therefore also by him, amen to God unto our 'glory."* [12] (The words in bold are emphasized with italics in the Douay-Rheims Bible)

Note how St. Paul is once again using a mysterious language, *"for our preaching which was to you, was not,* **It is***, and* **It is not***."* This is because St. Paul was indeed preaching that Jesus Christ is the Lord and Savior back when he wrote his epistles, however, to us *now*, in what he elsewhere refers to as *"due time,"*[13] St. Paul is preaching Jesus Christ according to the revelation of the mystery of Christ, the hidden knowledge of Christ he was given in the Third Heaven, which is now being unveiled.

Continuing the riddle, St. Paul writes, *"For the Son of God, Jesus Christ who was preached among you by us, by me and Sylvanus, and Timothy, was not,* **It is***, and* **It is not***, but,* **It is***, 'was in him.' For all the*

---

11 There is no past or future with God - there is only the eternal now. The power in the present moment when we enter into God's loving plan for our lives, His Divine Will, is so immense that it can transform us into His living image.

12 (2 Cor. 1:18-20) All Biblical quotes in this unveiling are taken from the Douay-Rheims Bible, a scrupulous word for word translation of the Latin Vulgate.

13 For example, in his letter to Titus St. Paul is speaking about the gospel committed to his trust when he writes, *But hath in due time [now] manifested his word in preaching, which is committed to me according to the commandment of God our Savior.*

promises of God are in Him, **It is**; *therefore also by him, amen to God 'unto our glory.''* Here St. Paul is making it known that the mystery has to do with God's Glory, God's Glory which *"was"* in the Son of God, but *"It is"* now in us—in whom Christ Jesus lives. St. Paul uses the word *"It"* to express the ineffable Glory of God.

In other words, the Glory of God which was in Jesus Christ is now in us and thus because He lives in us *"It is"* still in Him! The reason St. Paul is presenting the mystery in this manner will become clear as the hidden knowledge continues to unveil.

One of the most sublime mysteries we can fathom is that Jesus Christ truly lives in us. We should meditate on the profundity of this amazing grace every day of our lives—especially since it is our steadfast faith in His presence within us that is necessary to bring about all the promises of God's Glory.

St. Paul himself was first given a glimpse into the great mystery of Jesus' presence within Christians back when he was relentlessly persecuting the disciples of Jesus. This revelation was granted to him on his way to Damascus where he was going to bind Christian men and woman and bring them back to Jerusalem to be punished. As Paul, whose name was then Saul, drew near to Damascus, suddenly a bright light from Heaven shone around him, causing him, as well as his companions, to fall to the ground. At that time, he alone heard the voice of Jesus say to him, *"Saul, Saul, why persecutest thou me? And Saul answered, Who art thou, Lord? And he said to me: I am Jesus of Nazareth, whom thou persecutest.''* Jesus then instructed Saul who was blinded by the light to be led by his companions to Damascus. Meanwhile Jesus appeared in a vision to the Christian Ananias instructing him to heal Saul. Then Saul, after being unable to see for three days, received his healing and was baptized.

Having learned that he was indeed persecuting Jesus, into whose Mystical Body through the sacrament of Baptism Christians are truly incorporated, St. Paul would subsequently proclaim, *"And I live, now not I; but Christ liveth in me."* (Galatians 2:20) St. Paul would later pose the following question to deliberately test our faith in Christ Jesus' presence within us, *"Try your own selves if you be in the faith; prove ye yourselves. Know you not your own selves, that 'Christ Jesus' is in you, unless perhaps you be reprobates?"* (2 Corinthians 13:5)

To know that Christ Jesus is truly present within you is a marvelous and wonderful grace. Yet an even greater faith is needed to embrace the extraordinary knowledge of God contained in the unveiling of the mystery of Christ's Glory now being made known. Why is this so? Because, for example, to believe that since all the boundless treasures and riches of God's Glory are contained in His Son Jesus Christ, then, "hidden" within us, in whom He now dwells, would also be contained all the boundless treasures and riches of God's Glory. How incredibly amazing is this?

It was this very unveiling of the treasures and riches of Christ's Glory in us that St. Paul was shown when he was taken *"to the third heaven"* – *"caught up into paradise"* – our future, as seen in 2 Corinthians Chapter 12. Here in Scripture we read about how the visions and revelations of the Lord that St. Paul was shown were so great that he was given an angel of Satan to buffet him lest the greatness of the unveilings should exalt him!

To think: the hidden wisdom contained in the knowledge of God's Glory now being made known is so great that if Satan and his cohorts had known that God's Glory (through His Son's crucifixion) would be poured forth into us (through Baptism and the other six sacraments) they never would have crucified the Lord of Glory. St. Paul articulates it this way, *"But we speak the wisdom of God in a mystery, a wisdom which is hidden, which God ordained before the world, 'unto our glory;' which none of the princes of the world knew; for if they had known it, they would never have crucified 'the Lord of glory.' But, as it is written;* **That eye hath not seen, nor ear heard, neither hath it entered the heart of man, what things God hath prepared for them that love him.**" (I Corinthians 2:7-8) (The bold is emphasized with italics in the Douay-Rheims Bible.)

The power in the secret knowledge of God's Glory now being made known is so staggering that all the princes of this world (Satan and his cohorts) are no doubt shuddering in terror and anguish at its manifestation. In terror, because they know their time is nearing the end and their bitter pride and hideous hatred will soon be self-contained. In anguish, because they are insanely jealous of the glorious inheritance prepared for the meek and humble of heart who, living in God's infinite Love and Divine Will, embrace this knowledge.

Affirming that the revelation of the mystery now being manifested does in fact pertain to the riches of Christ's Glory hidden within us, St. Paul in Colossians 1:26-27 writes, *"The mystery which hath been hidden from ages and generations, but now is manifested to his saints to whom God would make known the riches of* **the glory of this mystery** *among the Gentiles, which* **is Christ, in you the hope of glory**."

Notice how when speaking of the Glory of this hidden mystery, St. Paul does not say that Christ is our hope of Glory, but rather, *"Christ 'in you' the hope of glory!"* Almost making it sound as if God's Glory depends on us.

The Unveiling of the Sons of God: As sons of God we are joint heirs of His Glory with Christ. However, in order for us to enter into the glorious inheritance God has prepared for us, there is an unequivocal stipulation—we must suffer with Jesus! St. Paul puts it this way:

> *"And if sons, heirs also; heirs indeed of God, and joint heirs with Christ; yet so, if we suffer with him, that we may be also glorified with him."* (Romans 8:17)

Then to spur us on towards the hope of the Glory to come, St. Paul continues:

> *"For I reckon that 'the sufferings of this time' are not worthy to be compared with* **'the glory to come, that shall be revealed in us'.** *For the expectation of the creature 'waiteth for the revelation of the sons of God."* (Romans 8:18-19)

First of all, the *"sufferings of this time"* that St. Paul is referring to are the sufferings of this last time, in which we are now living and through which the restoration of all things in Heaven and on earth are to come about.

Secondly, it is of utmost importance to note how St. Paul is comparing the Glory that is to be *"revealed in us"* with *"the revelation of the sons of God."* This connection is critical to grasp because this "awaited" revelation/unveiling of the sons of God is the very revelation/unveiling of Jesus Christ that St. Paul was shown in the Third Heaven—our future.

IN OTHER WORDS, THE REVELATION OF THE SONS OF GOD THAT ST. PAUL WAS SHOWN AND IS WRITING ABOUT IS: **THE UNVEILING OF JESUS CHRIST—AND ALL OF HIS GLORY—WITHIN US!!!**

Consequently, St. Paul's gospel is unique because it is the story of the life of Jesus Christ living within the great saints of this last time—the saints that we are all being called to become. Yes, people of all ages and from every nation, race, and walk of life are now, in a very special way through St. Paul's gospel, being called to become great saints. (This universal call to holiness announced by Vatican II and echoed by Saint John Paul II, is well depicted in a huge and beautiful display of art at the Basilica of the Immaculate Conception in Washington, D.C.)

Does this mean the saints of this last time become Jesus Christ? Well, no. However, it does mean that God is going to reveal His Son to them and in them, and that others will glorify God in them. Don't be so surprised. After all, this was foreseen by St. Paul who writes in Galatians: *"To reveal His Son in me"* (1:16); *"And they glorified God in me* (1:24)" [14]

These great saints, nurtured in God's charity are given the great grace to live in God's Divine Will so that through, with, and in them, God is able to ever so freely live, move, and have His being. Therefore, it is through these meek and humble instruments of God's Glory that He is able to bring His work of creation, redemption, sanctification and glorification into fulfillment.

This is a good place to reflect back to when Jesus' disciples were watching Him ascend into Heaven. Recall there were two men in white garments who appeared by Jesus saying: *"Ye men of Galilee, why stand you looking up to heaven? This Jesus who is taken up from you into heaven, so shall come, as you have seen Him going into heaven."* (Acts 1:11) This was spoken because we are not to look up for this coming of Jesus. We are not to look up because this coming of Jesus is the revelation—as in unveiling—of Jesus within us! This is the "Second Coming[15]" of Jesus not His "Third and final Coming" in the clouds of Heaven for which we are to look up as evidenced in Matthew 24:30 & Luke 21:27. Father Mary Joachim made this very clear to me.

---

14 Here it is good to contemplate the following: 1) St. Athanasius' famous teaching, "For the Son of God became man so that man might become god." 2) Jesus' words recorded in John 10:34, *"Is it not written in your law: 'I said you are gods?'"* 3) These extraordinary word's the priest, or deacon, silently prays at every Mass while preparing the wine for consecration, "By the mystery of this water and wine, may we come to share in the divinity of Christ who humbled himself to share in our humanity." 4) The metaphor of Christ as the sun, and we the rays of His light that shoot forth!

15 Perhaps the Church will choose to call this an intermediate or middle Coming of Christ, and continue to call His final coming in Glory the Second Coming. The author submits to the authority of the Church.

<u>The Long Suffering of Our Lord</u>: It was of this coming of Christ within us that Jesus was speaking when He said, *"In that day you shall know that I am in my Father, and you in me, and I in you."* (John 14:20)

When speaking of our faith in Jesus' presence within us, St. Paul corresponds this to the mystery of how we, like him, are called to suffer with Christ, *"For unto you it is given not only to believe in Him but also 'to suffer with Him'. Having the same conflict as that which you have seen in me, and now have heard of me."* (Philippians 1:29) Note how St. Paul writes that it is "given" to you not only to believe in Christ, but also to suffer with Him. This is because it is a "gift," we should treasure, to suffer with Christ. Paradoxically, the greater His gift, the more intense the suffering; this is seen in the lives of the saints to whom God has always entrusted the biggest crosses.

Our sufferings are measured and how we respond to them will correspond to the measure of our Glory to come. But let not your hearts be troubled because to suffer with Jesus brings an immensely deep consolation and intimacy never before experienced, of which many of the saints have written.[16] As does St. Paul when he writes, *"Hope; be steadfast: knowing that as you are partakers of the sufferings, so shall also you be of the consolation."* (2 Corinthians 1:7)

And so the preaching of Jesus Christ according to St. Paul's gospel not only makes known the secret knowledge of Christ's Glory hidden within us, but the means by which to attain His Glory—suffering.

Of course, this conquest can only be attained in God's Divine Will through a selfless, unconditional, and profound love of God

---

16 In the book <u>He and I</u> by Gabrielle Bossis, Jesus speaks: "And even before My passion, I knew what suffering was. I loved it for the love of you, My children. Love it for love of Me. I'll transform it into transformations for others, and into glory for you, since you find everything again in heaven. So take courage for suffering, My little children. There are some people who cannot do without suffering, so deeply have they experienced how close it brings them to Me. Although I love you unceasingly, I look with special love upon my children who suffer. My look is more tender, more affectionate than that of a mother. Of course, isn't it I who made the heart of a mother?" page 88 (bold added)

and one another. Jesus calls this love "agape." St. Paul describes this love as: *"A charity that beareth all things, believeth all things, hopeth all things, endureth all things."* (1 Corinthians 13:7)

For love of God and neighbor St. Paul's road to Glory was paved with countless persecutions and sufferings. For example, in 2 Corinthians 11:23-27 he tells us he was imprisoned; five times received forty stripes; three times was beaten by rods; stoned once; three times shipwrecked; spent a night and a day in the depths of the sea; and was often in perils, hungry, thirsty, naked, and cold. Emphasizing the merit of suffering St. Paul writes: *"For if we suffer we shall also reign with Him!"* (2 Timothy 2:12)

Throughout his epistles St. Paul writes about how we, like him, are called to suffer with Christ. St. Peter echoes this when he writes, *"And account the 'longsuffering' of our Lord, salvation; as also our most dear brother Paul, according to the wisdom given him, hath written to you: As also in all his epistles, speaking in them of these things[17]; in which are certain things hard to be understood, which the unlearned and unstable wrest, as they do also the other scriptures, to their own destruction."* (2 Peter 3: 15-16)

Consider in this verse how the word wisdom is being linked, once again, with the sufferings of the Lord. This is because the wisdom given St. Paul is the knowledge that God's plan for salvation necessarily involves suffering.

Next, ponder on how the sufferings of the Lord are referred to as being long. This is because included in the sufferings of our Lord and Savior Jesus Christ are His sufferings within Christians over the last 2000 years, and soon to culminate, in a most intense way, in the

---

17 "These things," per Father Joachim, are what St. Paul writes about as: *"the last days; the promise of His parousia [coming]; kept for fire in a day of judgment and destruction of ungodly men; the day of the Lord comes as a thief; the [present] heavens will pass away; the earth and its works be burned up; the Coming of the Day of the Lord; the heavens will be set on fire and dissolved; the elements will melt with fire."*

great saints of this last time.[18] But again, dear saints, be not afraid, because Jesus, who will both live and reign in you mystically, will not only shoulder your sufferings, He will turn them into the sweetest ecstasy. So let us not forget to unite our sufferings—mental, spiritual, and/or physical—with Jesus'.

Perhaps you're thinking, how is it possible that you can actually suffer with Jesus Christ who lived 2000 years ago? First consider that because there is no time or space with God, He sees everything that has happened, is happening, and will happen, in one glance. Next consider how we, who are in time, particularly in this last time, through our faith in Christ's presence within us will soon be "quickened" mystically into the very life, death, and resurrection of Jesus Christ Our Lord and Savior. Here's an example of how St. Paul explains it, *"But God, (who is rich in mercy) for his exceeding charity wherewith He loved us, even when we were dead in sins, **hath quickened us together in Christ.** [into His suffering, death, and resurrection] by whose grace you are saved, and hath raised us up together and hath made us sit together in the heavenly places, through Christ Jesus."* (Ephesians 2:4-6)

If you think about it, St. Paul never met Jesus Christ, nor was he at his crucifixion, yet he was able to proclaim: *"with Christ I am nailed to the cross"*;[19] and, *"I bear the marks of Jesus Christ in my body."*[20] St. Paul was able to proclaim this because he was quickened together with Jesus Christ—becoming one with Jesus Christ in Body and Spirit through Christ Jesus—the Mystical Body of Jesus Christ—the Church. Hence he was able to proclaim *"**have not I seen Christ Jesus our Lord?**"*[21]

---

18 19 Both St. Louis de Montfort and St. Therese of Lisieux have written that the saints of the last time would have more to suffer and correspondingly become greater saints.

19 Galatians 2:19

20 Galatians 6:17

21 1 Corinthians 9:1

In St. Paul's gospel, we, like him, are also being called to be quickened into the suffering, death and resurrection of Christ's Mystical Body.[22] Everything must come full circle.

Through the preaching of Jesus Christ, according to the unveiling of the hidden knowledge and wisdom now being made known, we will come to know and believe more and more in Jesus' presence within us. St. Paul is referring to this faith when he writes about *"the faith of Christ Jesus."*[23] It is through our faith in the presence of Christ Jesus within us, that we, like St. Paul, will come to know *"the power of His resurrection and the fellowship of His sufferings, being made conformable to His death."* [24] For if we are to rise with Him in Glory we must also suffer and die with Him!

An indication of growth in true intimacy with Jesus is a desire, which leads to an ardent longing, to be united with Him in His sufferings. St. Paul himself tells us that this word of the cross, our fellowship with His suffering, is a sign of predilection: *"For the word of the cross, to them indeed that perish, is foolishness; but to them that are saved, that is, to us, it is the power of God."* [25]

Wisdom, pay attention: The simplest way to grasp the mystery of Christ's long-suffering in St. Paul's epistles is to understand that everything that happened to Our Lord and Savior Jesus Christ is going to happen again to Christ Jesus—His Mystical Body. This is because our sufferings, like St. Paul's, are necessary to bring Christ's Mystical Body, the Church/us, into full stature.[26] If the servant is not

---

22 Some saints like St. Francis who lived in the 13th century and St. Pio who lived in the 20th century, have spent so much time at the foot of Jesus' cross that Jesus has allowed them to share in His passion in such a way that they have borne His Sacred wounds. We call this mystical union with Jesus the stigmata.

23 Philippians 3:9. (This explains how St. Augustine was able to write that there could not be faith "in" Jesus Christ, who is God.)

24 Philippians 3:10

25 I Corinthians 1:18

26 Colossians 1:24

greater than the master, and Jesus Himself had to suffer to enter into His Glory, then so too will we have to suffer to enter into His Glory.

The following quotation from the Old Covenant Book of Ecclesiastes 3:15, gives a concise explanation of the knowledge of God's Will for us in His plan of salvation:

> *"The things that shall be,*
> *have already been,*
> *and God restoreth that which is past."*

The interpretation is as follows:

* *"The things that shall be,"* which is to mean the life, passion, crucifixion, death and resurrection of **"Christ Jesus"**—the Mystical Body of Christ!
* *"have already been,"* which is to mean the life, passion, crucifixion, death and resurrection of **"Jesus Christ"**—Our Lord and Savior.
* *"and God restoreth that which is past"*, which is to mean that God will then restore Paradise, the Kingdom of His Divine Will to earth!

The Sacred Names Jesus Christ and Christ Jesus: The mystery of the Sacred Name Jesus Christ and its inversion Christ Jesus that is now being revealed, pertains to St. Paul's gospel and to the preaching of Jesus Christ according to what St. Paul calls the revelation of the mystery kept secret from eternity and *"now"* *"in due times"*—being manifested.

The preaching is that "everything" that happened to Our Lord and Savior Jesus Christ will happen again to His Mystical Body—Christ Jesus/God's people—in whom He lives, moves and has His being. This is necessary to bring all things into completion and perfection.

As we penetrate further into this mystery, we must keep in perspective that God's anointed priest sons are the "head" of His Mystical Body. This is important to understand because it is the head that directs the body. Therefore, in order for Christ's Mystical Body to enter into holiness, we need holy priests to shepherd it into holiness.

We will now delve deeper into the revelation of the mystery of this most glorious Coming of Christ within us that is now being unveiled. We begin with the understanding that the passion, death and resurrection of Christ Jesus will manifest first, foremost and most mightily through, with and in God's "Marian Priests." The lives of these holy priests are filled with selfless sacrifice, steadfast faith, total immersion in God's Divine Will, and true love and devotion to the Blessed Virgin Mary. These holy priests are most endeared to our Lord. They are the earthen vessels of Christ's Glory, the mediators between God and men that St. Paul is referring to in I Timothy 2:5-6 when he writes, *"For there is one God, and one mediator of God and men,* **the man Christ Jesus:** *Who gave himself a redemption for all,* **a testimony in due times."**

In Christ Jesus these Catholic priests are "one" in Body and Spirit with Jesus Christ. Thus, it is their—*testimony in due times*—that St. Paul was taken into the Third Heaven and shown. Consequently, it is their testimony that brings about the redemption of all: *"For all have sinned, and do need the glory of God. Being justified freely by his grace through* **the redemption that is in Christ Jesus."** (Romans 3:24) Then in 1 Corinthians 1:30-31 we read, **"But of Him are you in Christ Jesus,** *who of God is made unto us wisdom, and justice, and sanctification, and redemption: That, as it is written: He that glorieth, may glory in the Lord."* The redemption that is in Christ Jesus is *the redemption of our body* that St. Paul refers to in Romans 8:23.

Jesus' sanctification, like His glorification, came through suffering, as will the sanctification of God's beloved Marian Priest sons (who, by the way, will lead God's people/body down the same road to sanctification). St. Paul writes: **_And all that will live Godly in Christ Jesus shall suffer persecution._** [27] Here again, suffering is the hidden wisdom of the mystery St. Paul is speaking about when he writes: *"We speak the wisdom of God in a mystery, a wisdom hidden, unto our glory, otherwise they would not have killed the Lord of glory."* [28]

They never would have killed the Lord of Glory because it was precisely through His suffering and death that His Precious Blood, one with His Glory, is magnified and we come to share in "It!"

Our "redemption in Christ Jesus" comes to us through the precious Blood of Our Lord and Savior Jesus Christ. It is the precious Blood of Jesus Christ that gives life to Christ Jesus—His Mystical Body: *"In whom we have redemption through His blood, the redemption of sins, according to the riches of His grace."* (Ephesians 1:7) **_But now in Christ Jesus_**, *you, who some time were afar off, are made nigh by the blood of Christ."* (Ephesians 2:13) His precious Blood is what is bringing His Mystical Body/Christ Jesus into full stature.

In Leviticus 17:11 it is written: *"the life of the flesh is in the blood."* The application is the eternal life of our flesh—the redemption of our body—is in the Blood of Jesus Christ/Christ Jesus.

The very life of Jesus Christ through the Blood of His Cross has been entrusted to Christ Jesus—God's beloved priest sons. These are the earthen vessels in whom Jesus Christ has poured and hidden His Precious Blood. Through the seven sacraments our priests in the Person of Christ Jesus, the mediator of God and man, dispense God's precious Blood to God's people.

---

27 2 Timothy 3:12
28 I Corinthians 2:7

Once again, the life of Jesus Christ is soon to manifest out-wardly—through, with, and in Christ Jesus—God's beloved Marian priest sons. This manifestation is going to happen in such a way that everything that happened to Jesus Christ will happen again to them. This, as seen in Romans 8:24, is the *"hope"* we are *"saved by."*

As we go even deeper into the mystery, we must keep in perspective that St. Paul is seeing events from the viewpoint of the Third Heaven. Listen as he writes, *"Who is he that shall condemn?* **Christ Jesus that died, yea <u>that is risen also again</u>;** *who is at the right hand of God, who also maketh intercession for us."* (Romans 8:34) You see, in the realm of the eternal now, St. Paul is seeing God's beloved priest sons, in Christ Jesus, as having already been martyred and raised again in complete and perfect oneness with Jesus Christ.

In the remarkable book <u>To the Priests, Our Lady's Beloved Priest Sons</u>, Our Lady speaks, through messages given to Father Stephano Gobbi, to her beloved priest sons, "I will take you each day along the way of my Son, in such a way that He may increase in you to his fullness. This is my great work, which I am still carrying out in silence and in the desert. Under my powerful action as mediatrix of graces, 'you are ever more transformed into Christ, that you may become fit for the task which awaits you.' Forward then, with courage, along the way traced out by your heavenly Mother." (Message 204p)

In these profound messages the Sacred Name "Jesus Christ" appears eighty times, whereas Our Lady only mentions the Sacred Name "Christ Jesus" once, as follows: "The times have come when Jesus Crucified must be loved and glorified by you. Bring Him always with you and show Him to all as the only Savior and Redeemer. **'For this perverse generation of yours as well, there is no other possibility of salvation except in Christ Jesus Crucified."** (Message 393f) Bold added.

The glory of Christ Jesus will surely also manifest in other devout religious and lay people, but in lesser degrees of glory. For as St. Paul teaches there are different degrees of glory, i.e., *"one is the glory of the sun, another the glory of the moon, and another the glory of the stars. For star differeth from star in glory."* [29]

The Double Rainbow: Since God uses the visible (natural) to reveal His invisible (supernatural) plan, the following is a glimpse of how the beauty of a double rainbow mirrors God's Glory exemplified in the Sacred Names Jesus Christ and Christ Jesus.

First of all, consider how the seven colors of the rainbow covenant are a glorious reflection of the seven sacraments through which we enter into the Glory of God's Mystical Body.

Next, think about how in the first of the two rainbows the colors are always more vivid and brilliant. This primary rainbow would therefore represent the Glory of our Lord and Savior Jesus Christ coming down from Heaven.

Whereas in the second rainbow the colors are not only "inverted" but are also less vibrant. These colors can thus be likened to the Sacred Name Christ Jesus in whom the treasure of Christ's glory is presently obscured. This secondary rainbow would therefore represent God's Glory, through His beloved priest sons, who dispense His Glory to us, being returned to Heaven.

The double rainbow therefore reflects and signifies:

1. Our Lord and Savior **Jesus Christ** (the Son of God) who brought God's Glory down from Heaven leaving us the Church, flowing from the Precious Blood of His Sacred Heart, through which we come to partake of His Glory in the seven sacraments.

---

29 I Corinthians 15:41

2. Our priests in the Person of **Christ Jesus** (the sons of God) who through their holy anointing become earthen vessels of the Precious Blood—Christ's Glory, which they dispense to us through the seven sacraments of the Church.

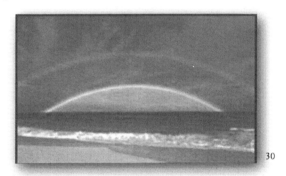

For this reason, Catholic priests in the Person of Christ Jesus, like St. Paul, are the ministers of Christ's precious Blood, His Glory, and the dispensers of the mysteries of God. Of God's anointed ministers St. Paul writes: *"Let a man so account of us as of the ministers of Christ, and the dispensers of the mysteries of God."* (I Corinthians 4:1)

As a dispenser of the mysteries of God, St. Paul understood that when he administered the sacraments he did so in the Person of Christ. This is evidenced when he pardoned the incestuous man who was repentant. St. Paul writes, *"For what I have pardoned, if I have pardoned anything, for your sakes I have done so in the Person of Christ. That we may not be overreached by Satan, for we are not ignorant of his devices."*

There is tremendous power when the priest, in the name of the Father and of the Son and of the Holy Spirit, absolves us from our sin. This power not only cleanses us of sin, it shields us against future attacks by Satan and also fortifies us to resist committing future sin. It is for this reason that St. Paul advises us not to be ignorant

30 Angelina Hills Photography

of the many stumbling blocks that Satan will trip us with to keep us from partaking of this awesome treasure of God's glory.

Dear ones, as you contemplate this great mystery of faith keep in mind that there is no past or future with God, because He lives in the "eternal now"—the present moment. When we enter into the present moment we, like St. Paul, are able to enter into the very life and humanity of His Son Jesus Christ.

Prayers prayed, words said, and deeds done in God's Divine Will have eternal value and tremendous power, because, like Jesus', they affect all generations, past, present and future. God, in a very special way, is calling us now to leave our past to His mercy, our future to His providence, and to live the present moment immersed in His Infinite Love[31] and Divine Will. (When our thoughts, words, actions, and deeds are selfish, greedy, prideful, jealous, hateful, lustful, envious, and unforgiving, we literally choke and suffocate Jesus who lives in us. Mortal sin crucifies Him.)

Since the things that shall be, have already been, perhaps you're wondering where our humanity is now mystically joined with the humanity of our Lord and Savior Jesus Christ in the line of time and space. The answer is the last 2000 years were representative of Jesus Christ's hidden life on earth, and we are soon to enter into Jesus' public life which lasted three and a half years. If you recall, Jesus' public life began at the wedding feast of Cana, where Jesus in obedience to His Mother Mary's request transformed six jugs of water into wine *"and manifested His glory. And his disciples believed in Him."* (John 2:11)

---

31 To strengthen and fortify us in the Love of Christ, St. Paul encourages us: *Above all things to clothe ourselves in love; to let all that we do be done in love; to be rooted and grounded in love* (Ephesians 3:17); *with patience to bear with one another with love* (Ephesians 4:2); *to be of one mind with him, having the same love, being of one accord, agreeing in sentiment; to pursue righteousness, faith, love, and peace* (Philippians 2:2); and, *to know the love of Christ that surpasses all knowledge* (Ephesians 3:19). The love of Christ surpasses all knowledge because it not only transcends, but transforms all things – making them anew.

When you think about it, over the last 2000 years a similar miracle has been perpetuated at the Wedding Feast of the Lamb—the Holy Sacrifice of the Mass. Here priests, in the Person of Christ, have been taking bread and wine and transforming (transubstantiating) it into the precious Body and Blood of Jesus Christ.

<u>Marian Priests</u>: Keeping in perspective that the things that shall be, have already been, we can foretell that soon at this Wedding Feast God will again manifest His Glory visibly – when at the hands of Marian Priests, priests strongly devoted to Mary, many amazing miracles will take place. For example, some people will see glorious rays of light[32] emanating from the consecrated Host and/or Precious Blood, while others will see Jesus Himself manifest in the consecrated Host and Precious Blood, and still others will see the priest become the Person of Jesus Christ. These wondrous miracles will illuminate the hearts and minds of countless people who will come to believe in the true presence of Jesus Christ in the Host and Precious Blood—as well as in the Priest.

The Marian Priests, through whose hands these miracles are wrought, will have embraced and preached St. Paul's gospel of the Glory of Christ. These holy, devout, and merciful priests, soon to be sanctified, will shepherd the faithful into holiness. In this last

---

32 ***In the book <u>To the Priests Our Lady's Beloved Sons</u>, which contains messages from our Lady to Fr. Stefano Gobbi, Our Lady speaks, "Because in the Eucharist Jesus Christ is really present, He remains ever with you and this presence of His will become increasingly stronger, will shine over the whole earth like a sun and will mark the beginning of a new era. The coming of the glorious reign of Christ will coincide with the greatest splendor of the Eucharist. Christ will restore his glorious reign in the universal triumph of his Eucharistic reign, which will unfold in all its power and will have the capacity to change hearts, soul, individuals, families, society and the very structure of the world. When He will have restored His Eucharistic reign, Jesus will lead you to take joy in this habitual presence of His, which you will feel in a new and extraordinary way and which will lead you to the experience of a second, renewed and more beautiful earthly paradise. Message 360: v & w.

time their light will grow brighter – and the dark will become more gruesome and beastly.

The three and a half years of Jesus' public life will literally correspond to three and a half[33] years of time as we know it (corresponding to the time the two Olive Trees will prophecy, as seen in Revelation 11). Recall the miracles and wonders wrought by Jesus as well as His apostles and disciples during His public life. Likewise, many mighty miracles and great wonders will soon abound at the hands of Marian Priests, as well as by other devout deacons, religious and lay people. It was in part of these wonders yet to take place that Jesus was speaking when He said, *"Amen, Amen I say to you, he that believeth in Me, the works that I do, he also shall do, and greater than these shall he do."* (John 14:12)

Dear saints, all the luminous events in Jesus' life will be manifested again. This is precisely why Saint John Paul II, great prophet that he was, gave us the Luminous Mysteries of the rosary to pray. Through meditating on these luminous times in the life of Jesus we are being given the grace to literally enter into oneness – quickened – with Jesus' humanity as He lived and walked these very mysteries on earth.

The Blessed Mother has been known to say that the New Era of Peace will come to the earth through the praying of the rosary[34]. Jesus was obedient to His Mother's request. We, like Jesus, are being asked to lovingly submit to His Mother's request to pray the rosary daily. When we truly embrace praying the rosary with

---

33 This three and a half year period also corresponds with the seven day (to be equated to seven years) peace covenant foretold in Daniel 9:27. This covenant fails (is broken) half way through (three and a half years), at which time, according to Daniel, the abomination of desolation is set up in the temple. Daniel writes, *and the desolation shall continue even to the consummation, and to the end.* Jesus refers to this abomination of desolation in Matthew 24:15-16; Mark 13:14; and Luke 21:20-21.

34 St. Dominic prophesied that the world would be saved through the Rosary and the Brown Scapular.

our hearts we will be given the grace to enter into the present moment, in which dwells God's Divine Will, wherein we shall become mystically united with Jesus and Mary in the joyful, luminous, sorrowful and glorious times in their lives. Ask, or, better yet, beg God to give you the desire to pray the rosary daily and He will not refuse you.

During Jesus' public life He also experienced much ridicule, persecution, and betrayal, all of which led to His passion, crucifixion and death and all of which will also happen again. The culmination of these events in the life of Jesus Christ, portrayed in the Sorrowful Mysteries of the rosary, will take place again on Mt. Zion where 144,000[35] celibate virgins (Marian Priests) hold a most sacred Marian Cenacle—in complete union and oneness with Jesus at the Last Supper. Afterwards, these Marian Priests, quickened into oneness with Jesus, the Lamb of God, knowingly and willingly are led like lambs to the slaughter.[36] These are God's "little lambs"—they are living replicas, perfect images of Jesus Christ.[37]

---

35 Revelation 14::1-5: *And I beheld, and lo a lamb stood upon mount Zion, and with him an hundred forty-four thousand, having his name, and the name of his Father, written on their foreheads (vs.1). These are they who were not defiled with woman; for they are virgins.* <u>*These follow the Lamb withersoever he goeth.*</u> *These were purchased from among men, the firstfruits to God and to the Lamb (vs. 4). And in their mouth there was found no lie; for they are without spot before the throne of God (vs.5).* This number 144,000, represents a third of Catholic Priests in the world; another third of the Catholic Priests will convert when they witness the testimony their brother priests give on Mt. Zion; the final third are the fallen stars mentioned in Revelation 12:4, "*and his [the great red dragon] tail drew the third of the fallen stars from heaven.* (Wisdom pay attention: Three times 144,000 equal 434,000. The Catholic Church presently has approximately 420,000 priests with numbers increasing.)

36 In December 2008 crucifixion was made legal again by Muslim law.

37 The following quotation is taken from within Hugh Owen's book <u>New and Divine: The Holiness of the Third Christian Millennium</u>, "To the Venerable Conchita, Our Lord said '**I want to return to the world in My priests...I want to give a mighty impulse to my Church infusing in her, as it were, a new Pentecost, the Holy Spirit, in My priests.** May the whole world have recourse to this Holy Spirit since the day of his reign has arrived. This last stage of the world belongs very specially to Him that He be honored and exalted..." page 158

This Passover, the Church's ultimate trial, is depicted in Section 677 of the Catechism of the Catholic Church: "The Church will enter the glory of the kingdom only through this final Passover when she will follow her Lord in his death and Resurrection. The Kingdom will be fulfilled, then, not by a historic triumph of the Church through a progressive ascendency, but only by God's victory over the final unleashing of evil, which will cause his Bride to come down from Heaven. God's triumph over the revolt of evil will take the form of the Last Judgement after the final cosmic upheaval of this passing world."

It is very telling that in the mouths of these little lambs is found *"no lie,"* see Revelation 14:5, this is because they will have preached St. Paul's Gospel of *"Truth"* – now being manifested!

The Manifestation of Truth: Throughout Chapter 4 of St. Paul's second letter to the Corinthians he is instructing us that his gospel, his revelation of Jesus Christ, comes to us *"by manifestation of the truth."* (vs. 2). Of this Manifestation of Truth, he writes, *"And if our gospel be also hid, it is hid to them that are lost... that 'the light of the knowledge of the gospel of the glory of Christ,' who is the image of God, should not shine unto them."* (vs. 3-4) St. Paul then instructs us that the light of the knowledge of the Glory of God is *"in the face of Christ Jesus."* (vs. 6) The face being in the "head," and the head of God's Mystical Body is, as we have seen, God's beloved priest sons.

As we further reflect on these meaningful verses we are able to deduce that since Jesus is the Truth, the Manifestation of Truth St. Paul is writing about is the manifestation of Jesus. Jesus, whose manifestation in Glory, per St. Paul, will be "hid: from the eyes of those who are lost. However, those who accept and believe in the Gospel of Christ's Glory, when it is preached by the Church, can anticipate seeing and experiencing this manifestation of light in the face of Christ Jesus—God's most cherished and beloved Priest Sons.

St. Paul goes on to tell us that he and his disciples have this trea-sure of Christ's Glory *"in earthen vessels, that its excellence may be of the power of God and not of them."* (vs. 7) He then emphasizes in the next four verses that this treasure of Christ's Glory manifested in them through tribulation, persecution, being cast down, and other sufferings. For example, he writes: *"Always bearing about in our body the mortification of Jesus; that the life also of Jesus may be made manifest in our bodies. For we who live are always delivered unto death for Jesus' sake; that the life also of Jesus may be made 'manifest in our mortal flesh. So then death worketh in us, but life in you."* (vs. 10-12)

These verses are also very meaningful because in the same way the sufferings of Jesus' life manifested in St. Paul and his disciples, so too will they manifest again, first and foremost, in God's coura-geous Marian Priest sons. This suffering takes place when they, like St. Paul, preach the light of the knowledge of the Gospel of the Glory of Christ!

This chapter ends with St. Paul emphasizing again that the Gospel of the Glory of God is made manifest through the crucible of suffering, *"For that which is at present momentary and light of our tribulation, worketh for us above measure exceedingly 'an eternal weight of glory."* [38] *"For I think God hath set forth us apostles, the last, as it were men appointed to death: we are made a spectacle to the world, to angels, and to men."* [39] You see, because St. Paul was *"born out of due time"* his preaching and suffering is, in a more specific way, to be an aspira-tion for the present day priests—the last apostles. The actualization of their destiny (their quickening into Jesus' life, passion, death and resurrection) brings all things in Heaven and earth into fullness/fruition. This is how St. Paul is able to include himself with the apostles, our priests, of this last time.

---

38 1 Corinthians 4:9

39 *And last of all, He was seen also by me, as by one born out of due time.* I Corinthians 15:8

We'll come back to the meaningful way St. Paul labels their reward *"an eternal weight of glory!"*

<u>Fellowship with St. Paul's sufferings</u>: Like St. Paul, God's beloved priest sons contain the treasures of Christ's Glory in their earthen vessels. Thus, this Manifestation of Truth—the Gospel of the Glory of Christ—is about how they, like St. Paul, are called to fill up *those things* that are wanting of the sufferings of Christ, in the flesh, for Christ's Body, the Church, as seen in Colossians 1:24. St. Paul writes about "those things" in all of his letters including Philippians 1:29 where he explicitly states, *"For unto you it is given for Christ, not only to believe in Him, but also to suffer for Him. Having the same conflict as that which you have seen in me, and have heard of me."*

In I Corinthians 1:2-6 St. Paul is writing to those who are soon to be "sanctified in Christ Jesus, called to be saints," about *"the testimony of Christ"* (the sufferings) that is to be confirmed in them. These are those, he says, who in grace are *"waiting for the manifestation of our Lord Jesus Christ"* (vs. 7); they are the called: *"God is faithful by whom you are called unto the fellowship of his Son Jesus Christ our Lord."* (vs. 9)

The fellowship with the Son of God that the sons of God are now being called to is clearly with His suffering, as seen in St. Paul's letter to the Philippians 3:10-11: *"That I may know Him, and the power of his resurrection, <u>and the fellowship of his sufferings,</u> being made conformable to his death, if by any means I may attain to the resurrection which is from the dead."*

We see here, yet again, that in order for the life of Jesus to manifest in our midst, our witness to Christ inevitably involves persecution, mortification and suffering. In other words, the cross! Further on in this chapter of Philippians St. Paul insists and persists in preaching his gospel—the Mystery of Christ's passion and cross: *"For Christ sent me not to Baptize, but to preach 'the gospel'; not in wisdom of speech, lest 'the cross of Christ' should be made void. For 'the word of the cross,' to them indeed that perish, is foolishness; but to them that are saved, that is to us, it is the power of God (vs. 17-18).* A few verses later he writes: *For both the Jews require signs, and the Greeks seek after wisdom, but 'we preach Christ crucified,' unto the Jews indeed a stumbling block, and unto the Gentiles foolishness, that is, to us, it is the power of God."* (vs.22) St. Paul's preaching of Christ, his gospel, is all about the Word of the Cross – Christ crucified. In section 675 of the CCC we see where this final trial the Church must pass through, will shake the faith of many believers.

The Word of Truth, the Gospel of our Salvation: The destiny of God's heroic Marian Priest sons is brought about through their preaching St. Paul's gospel, the Gospel of Christ's Glory." In Ephesians 1:13 St. Paul refers to it as *"the word of truth—the gospel of our salvation."*

It is insightful that when St. Paul mentions the Word of Truth, the gospel of our salvation, in I Timothy 2;4-5, he calls it *"the knowledge of truth"* to which the man Christ Jesus is to give testimony in due times: **"For there is one God, and one mediator of God and men, 'the man Christ Jesus': Who gave himself a redemption for all, a testimony in due times."** This verse is very enlightening because in it Saint Paul is using both past and future tense in the same sentence when speaking of Christ Jesus, as he writes: "Christ Jesus 'gave' himself a redemption for all, a testimony in 'due times." Dear saints, St. Paul is in the mystery of the things that shall be, have already been!

<u>The Eternal Gospel</u>: Regarding this testimony that is yet to take place, St. Paul next writes: *"Where unto I am appointed a preacher and an apostle, (I say the <u>'truth</u>,' I <u>lie</u> not,) a doctor of the Gentiles in faith and 'truth." (vs. 2:7)* Observe here how St. Paul makes a point of stating **I say the truth, I lie not,"** thus connecting His Gospel of the Knowledge of Truth to the 144,000 virgins of the Book of Revelation 14:5 *"in whose mouth there was found **no lie!**"* In the mouth of these virgins is found no lie because they preach the Knowledge and Word of Truth.

This Manifestation of Truth, once again, is the manifestation of Christ Jesus in God's true and faithful Marian Priest sons. The luminous light of God's Glory is to shine ever so brightly in their faces when they preach the Knowledge of Truth, the light of the Gospel of the Glory of Christ.

Wisdom, be attentive: This Manifestation of the knowledge of Truth, the Gospel of Christ's Glory, is the "eternal Gospel" St. John in the Book of Revelations 14:6 sees the angel flying through the midst of Heaven with: *"And I saw another angel flying through the midst of heaven, having 'the eternal gospel' to preach to them that sit upon the earth, and over every nation, and tribe, and tongue, and people."* This *Eternal Gospel* is called such because it carries with it *"an exceedingly above measure 'eternal weight of glory."* Scripture interprets Scripture!

Everything must come full circle, hence the Gospel of the Kingdom of God's Glory that Jesus Christ, Our Lord and Savior, preached is the same Eternal Gospel of Christ's Glory that is reflected in the Third Luminous Mystery of the rosary—The Preaching of the Kingdom, of God's Glory.

In complete and sacred oneness with Jesus, as well as with St. Paul and his disciples, the Gospel of the Kingdom of God's Glory will be preached "again" by God's beloved Marian Priest sons. This proclamation of the Kingdom of God's Glory brings about the Manifestation of Truth, Jesus in them, this is the Second Coming of Jesus (or intermediate coming of Jesus!). In praying and meditating on this Mystery of Light—the Third Luminous Mystery of the rosary—we, along with God's Marian Priest sons, are entering into the very mystery and bringing it into fruition: *"Calleth those things that are not, as though they are."* (Romans 4:17) These are the very works that God has prepared for His beloved priest sons and people to walk in: *"For we are His workmanship,* **created in Christ Jesus** *in good works, which God hath prepared that we should walk in them."* (Ephesians 2:10)

It is also worth noting, the virginity and celibacy of Jesus Christ represents His courageous detachment from "all" the things of this world. This same detachment, which brings peace beyond our understanding, is a virtue gifted to His 144,000 most cherished Marian Priests.

The Gospel of Truth: We are sanctified through Jesus, who is the Word of Truth, the gospel of our salvation. In John 17:17-19, just prior to Jesus' passion and death, he prays to the Father asking that his disciples be sanctified in truth: *"As thou has sent me into the world, I also have sent them into the world. And for them do I sanctify myself, that they also may be* <u>*sanctified in truth.*</u>*"*

St. Paul boldly exclaims that it is according to the dispensation of God's Will that his ministry, his gospel, will *"fulfill the word of God."*[40] This is possible because the preaching of God's Kingdom of Glory according to St. Paul's gospel brings about the restoration of all things in Heaven and on earth in Jesus Christ/Christ Jesus.

---

40 Colossians 1:25

On May 25, 1993 the Blessed Mother was speaking of this Manifestation of Truth when she told Josyp Terelya, a great mystic and prophet of our time, the following: "A great cross has been prepared for me in this last time—how few there are who are awaiting the manifestation of the gospel of truth."[41] (Underline added)

Let us pray in God's Divine Will, that the eyes of all Catholic as well as our non-Catholic brethren are opened to the Gospel of Truth, the Gospel of the Glory of Christ, the Eternal Gospel now being unveiled and soon to be preached by God's most cherished and beloved Marian Priest sons.

"THE MYSTERY OF GOD THE FATHER AND OF CHRIST JESUS"

Comforting us with the knowledge of how very much we are loved, St. Paul desires we come to the full understanding of the great mystery of God the Father and of Christ Jesus, now being unveiled, of which he writes: *"That their hearts may be comforted, being instructed in charity, and unto all riches of fullness of understanding, unto the knowledge of 'the mystery of God the Father and of Christ Jesus,': in whom are hid all the treasures of wisdom and knowledge."* (Colossians 2:2)

The great mystery of God the Father and of Christ Jesus pertains to God's beloved priest sons, God's earthen vessels of Glory in whom are hid all the treasures of wisdom and knowledge. The Great Mystery is that God's beloved priest sons, in Christ Jesus, are "one" with God the Father. This, dear saints, is precisely why we call them "FATHER!" In them dwells the fullness of the God-head, as seen in Colossians 2:9: *"For in them dwelleth the fullness of the 'Godhead'*

---

41 Josyp Terelya, In the Kingdom of the Spirit, page 68.

corporeally [bodily]." Recollecting Jesus' words to Philip, *"Philip, he that seeth me seeth the Father also."* (John 14:9)

As the head of the Church, our priests, like St. Paul, are building up the body (God's people) of Christ—the Church. They have been given this authority through their anointing which has been passed from the very hands of Jesus Christ onto the Apostles and down the ages to our present-day priests. This powerful chain of grace has never been broken.

At the Last Supper Jesus bequeathed to His Apostles—and to the priests who would follow in their footsteps, the Kingdom of His Glory. The very Kingdom of His Glory God the Father bestowed on Him, as evidenced in His words, *"And I dispose to you, as my Father hath disposed to me, a kingdom."* (Luke 22:29) In the last discourse we hear Jesus praying to the Father for the Apostles, *"And the 'glory' which thou hast given me, I have given to them, that they may be one, as we also are one. I in them, and thou in me, that they may be made perfect in 'one."* (John 17:22-23) What a marvel, the very Kingdom of God and all its treasures and riches of Glory have been entrusted to God's holy priest sons, the ministers of the mysteries!

In the following passage St. Paul wishes to clarify that being a Father in the Church is fundamentally different from being an instructor. In making the distinction, he professes to give birth to the gospel of Christ Jesus now being manifested: *"For if you have ten thousand instructors in Christ, yet not many 'fathers.' **For in 'Christ Jesus,' by 'the gospel' I have begotten you**."* (I Corinthians 4:15)

Of course, the role of an instructor cannot compare with that of our devout, faithful, and virtuous Church Fathers. These, our spiritual priestly Fathers, are rooted and grounded in the faith and charity that is in Christ Jesus, *"Now the grace of our Lord hath abounded exceedingly with **faith and love, which is in Christ Jesus**."* [42] They lavishly bestow

42 1Timothy 1:14

God's peace, love, mercy, grace, and glory on us. Their great capacity to love, like Jesus', surpasses all knowledge and understanding. They, like Jesus, lay down their lives for us. St. Paul gives birth to, as in begets, them through his gospel of Christ's Glory now being manifested. The knowledge and wisdom contained in St. Paul's Gospel of the Glory of Christ gives great depth to their vocation and ministry.

Please understand that as noble and gratifying the calling to become a biological father is, the call to enter into the Fatherhood of a Catholic priest is of the highest degree of nobility, and the rewards are vastly more gratifying in this life as well as in the next. Jesus Himself tells us so, recall when Simon Peter, on behalf of himself as well as the other apostles, commented to Jesus, *"Behold, we have left all things, and have followed thee. To which Jesus responded, Amen, I say to you, there is no man who has left house, or parents, or brethren, or wife, or children, for the Kingdom of God's sake, who shall not receive more in this present time, and in the world to come, life everlasting."* (Matthew 18:28-30)

Furthermore, the joy and intimacy of a devout priest's deep spiritual relationship with Jesus far exceeds that of the conjugal act between a husband and wife, as beautiful as this may be. Unfortunately, the sensual man is not able to perceive the kind of heightened intimacy and spirituality that characterizes the Catholic priesthood. Alas, the sensual person also projects onto others his own inferior level of thinking. Comparing the outlook of the spiritual person to that of the sensual one, St. Paul writes: *"But the sensual man perceiveth not these things that are of the Spirit of God; for it is foolishness to him, and he cannot understand, because it is spiritually examined. But the spiritual man judgeth all things; and he himself is judged of no man."*[43]

Spiritually examined, just as Jesus' glorification came about through His being betrayed and His cross, so too will the glorification

---

43 I Corinthians 2:14

of God's true and faithful priests come about through their being betrayed and through their cross. This is why St. Paul insists on preaching Christ and Christ crucified in season and out of season. Recall that it was immediately after Judas' betrayal that Jesus entered into His hour of darkness saying, *"Now is the Son of Man glorified, and God is glorified in Him. If God be glorified in Him, God also will glorify Him in Himself; and immediately will He glorify Him."* (John 13:31-32) The deepest darkness comes before the dawn of the new day.

As you contemplate the following prayer penned by St. Paul nearly 2000 years ago, note how he is asking "the Father of Glory" to give us the spirit of wisdom and revelation in the knowledge of God, now being unveiled in fullness, *"That the God of our Lord Jesus Christ, 'the Father of glory', may give unto you the spirit of 'wisdom and revelation, in the knowledge of him': The eyes of your heart enlightened, that you may know what the hope is of his calling, and what are the riches of the glory of his inheritance in the saints."* [44]

This prayer penned and prayed so long ago is now being fully answered as follows:

1. The "spirit of wisdom" is: the knowledge in the necessity of suffering to bring God's plan of salvation into perfection and completion.
2. The "spirit of revelation" is: the revelation of the Mystery of Christ's Second Coming (or Intermediate Coming), which is to take place through, with and in Christ Jesus – God's holy and beloved Marian Priest Sons (the revelation of the sons of God) and also in those who follow in their footsteps.
3. The "knowledge of Him" is: the full knowledge of Our Lord and Savior Jesus Christ herein being manifested.

---

44 Ephesians 1:17-18

"The knowledge of Him," entails the full means by which we become partakers of Christ's Glory through His Church—His Mystical Body. This knowledge of the riches of Christ's Glory is so very sacred that it has been kept secret, remained a mystery, until now—the fullness of times[45].

The unveiling of this knowledge which was hidden and is now, in due time, being manifested is "the Gospel of the Glory of Christ" committed to St. Paul's trust, and of which he writes:

* *"Which is according to the gospel of the glory of the blessed God committed to my trust."* (Timothy 1:11)
* *"Whereunto he hath called you by our gospel, unto the purchasing of the glory of Christ."* (II Thessalonians 2:13)

---

45 In the book <u>Salt of the Earth – The End of the Present Millennium</u>, Joseph Cardinal Ratzinger, our Pope Emeritus, was asked to interpret what Pope, now Saint, John Paul II meant when he spoke about "the fullness of times" in his apostolic letter *Tertio Millenio Adveniente*, and also what John Paul II meant when he said: "that the concept of time has a 'fundamental importance' in Christianity. With the coming of Christ, in fact, the 'last days', the 'last hour' has already begun. The 'time of the Church, which will last until the Parousia', begins now." Cardinal Ratzinger's answer, in part, follows, "I would say that the development of the last decades, with the acceleration of world history and with its growing threat, has brought the idea of the end of time much more sharply into the field of vision again. Not only that. We also understand in a new way that, as a matter of fact, with the Christian movement – which from the beginning aims at world unification, in some way at the separation of Church and state, and introduces a certain autonomy by de-divinizing the world – that with Christianity a new and in some sense definitive phase of history has begun. This phase of history is marked by the awareness that the end of history is approaching, not according to calculations of millennia, but that history is on the way, and that Christ is, as it were, the end that has begun, and that the world, while moving away from Him, is nonetheless moving toward Him again." Cardinal Ratzinger continues, "This is what the Pope [John Paul II] is talking about, that Christ brings the decisive milestone into world history itself and that, in the uncertainties of history, which are becoming ever more dramatic, he remains not only the point of departure but also the destination. Oriented toward Him, we are on our way to an end. An end that is not simply destruction but is consummation, which brings history to an inner totality. (pages 277 & 278)

❖ *"In whom the god of this world hath blinded the minds of unbeliev-*
ers, that the light of the gospel of the glory of Christ, who is the
image of God, should not shine unto them." (2 Corinthians 4:4)

A good place to begin to seek out this hidden, or secret, knowledge
of God's Glory now being revealed is in the Old Covenant throughout which God often reveals His Glory in "the Cloud of His Glory."
For example:

❖ *"And when Aaron spoke to all the assembly of the children of Israel,*
they looked towards the wilderness: and behold the glory of the Lord
appeared in a cloud." (Exodus 16:10)

❖ *"Nor could the priests stand and minister by reason of the cloud.*
For the glory of the Lord had filled the house of God." (II
Paralipomenon/Chronicles 5:14)

❖ *"Give ye glory to the God of Israel, His magnificence and power is*
in the clouds." (Psalm 67:35)

❖ *"Moses and Aaron fled to the tabernacle of the covenant. And*
when they were gone into it, the cloud covered it, and the glory of
the Lord appeared." (Numbers 16:42)

(In the book <u>The Life of Christ</u>, Blessed Catherine Emmerich describes Abraham's reception of the Old Covenant sacrament: "Then
with both hands the angel held something like a little 'luminous
cloud' toward Abraham's breast. I saw it entering him, and I felt as if
he was receiving the Blessed Sacrament."[46])

It is very telling that in the Old Covenant, which is a foreshadowing of the New Covenant, God chose to reveal His magnificence and power—His Glory—in a Cloud. This is exceedingly
profound because the very two elements of a "pure cloud" are

---

46 Blessed Anne Catherine Emmerich, <u>The Life of Christ,</u> Vol. I, p. 85.

"water and salt" which just so happen to be the very two elements through which we enter into the Mystical Body of Christ in Baptism.

Sister and Brothers, through the fascinating knowledge and understanding of these two meek and humble "substance" of Christ's Glory, water and salt, the Gospel of the Glory of Christ is being unveiled and shall be prophesied[47] "...*again to many nations, and peoples, and tongues, and kings.*"

"For we are made partakers of Christ:

yet so,

if we hold the beginning of His 'substance' firm unto the end."

(HEBREWS 3:1)

---

47 Revelations 10:11

CHAPTER 2

"For there is nothing hid which shall not be made manifest,
neither was it made secret,
but that it may come abroad."

MARK 4:22

The Rise of God's Kingdom into Wholeness

The Parable of the Three Measures of Meal

JESUS WAS PREACHING TO THE multitudes from a boat off the shores of the Sea of Galilee when he told the following powerful parable on the Kingdom of Heaven and its rise into wholeness:

> *"The Kingdom of Heaven is like to leaven, which a woman took*
> *and hid in three measures of meal, until the whole was leavened."*

(MATTHEW 13:33)

The full knowledge and understanding of the meaningful mystery contained in this parable is now being revealed because the Kingdom of Heaven, like the woman's three measures of meal, is "now" rising into wholeness.

The Three Measures of Meal: First of all, the three measures of meal have always been understood to represent three measures of bread dough that are "hidden under a veil" as they rise into wholeness—this is typically how bread dough rises.

And since it takes "a period of time" for the "veiled" bread dough to rise into wholeness, these measures of hidden bread dough can therefore be likened to the hidden bread—as in the "hidden manna"—given to those who persevere in "the last time" at the rising of God's Kingdom into wholeness. God is speaking of this hidden bread in the Book of Revelation when He instructs St. John to write, *"To him that overcometh [the last time tribulations] I will give the 'hidden manna'..."* (Revelation 2:17)

The word manna reminds us of the bread come down from Heaven on which the Israelites were fed in the desert for 40 years. This manna was a foreshadowing of Jesus the Bread of Eternal Life who came down from Heaven and remains with us hidden in the consecrated Bread—the Eucharistic Meal.

Also note in the parable how Jesus uses the analogy of "three" measures of bread in the "one" meal. This is because when we eat the Bread of Everlasting Life, we are partaking of all three Divine Persons in one God—the Father, the Son and the Holy Spirit—the whole Trinity.

For these reasons Jesus' true, real, and substantial presence hidden in the Eucharistic Bread is both the veiled bread Jesus is referring to in the parable as well as the hidden manna St. John is referring to in the Book of Revelation.

The Rising of Bread Dough takes place under a Veil—Without Observation: Please ponder the profound meaning of the following: Since Jesus is the risen Bread of Life, then those who eat this Bread—because they have not as yet risen into wholeness—are to be likened to the "veiled bread dough" in the parable. This is because when we eat Jesus in the Eucharistic Bread—His Kingdom, like the veiled bread dough, <u>is veiled within us and rising unseen</u>!

And so, we can see that this parable is ultimately about the rising of God's Kingdom "veiled within us" into wholeness. This is why when the Pharisees asked Jesus: *"when the Kingdom of God should come? He answered them, and said: The Kingdom of God* [48] **cometh not with observation***: Neither shall they say: Behold here, or behold there.* **For lo, the Kingdom of God is within you***."* (Luke 17:20-21)

The Unveiling of the Bread Dough, Jesus within Us—Comes with Observation: The rising of the bread dough, like the rising of Christ Jesus within us, is without observation—that is, until it rises into wholeness at which time the unveiling of the bread dough— Christ Jesus within us—takes place.

Wisdom, Pay Attention: The unveiling of the bread dough, which comes with observation, is the unveiling of the sons of God that St. Paul is referring to when he writes: *"For the expectation of the creature waiteth for the revelation of the sons of God."* (Romans 8:9). You see, since the word revelation is synonymous with the word unveiling—and the sons of God are to be equated with the veiled bread dough in the parable, this verse could very well read, *For the expectation of the creature waiteth for* <u>*the unveiling of the bread dough!*</u>

Jesus was speaking of this unveiling of Himself within us when He said: *"In that day you shall know that I am in my Father, and you in me, and I in you."* (John 13:20) How will we know this? In that day, soon to come, the Glory of Christ veiled within us is going to be unveiled and shine outwardly for the entire world to see. It was of this day, soon to come, that Jesus spoke to the Father saying, *"And the 'glory' which thou has given me, I have given to them; that they may be one, as we are also one: I in them, and thou in me; that they may be made*

---

48 All Biblical quotations throughout this unveiling of Sacred Scripture are taken from the Douay-Rheims Bible – an authentic Word for Word translation of St. Jerome's Latin Vulgate. Some of the new and revised versions have taken us away from the fullness of Truth.

perfect in one: and the world may know that thou has sent me, and hast loved them, as thou hast also loved me." (John 17:22-23).

After the unveiling of the bread dough (the revelation of the sons of God that St. Paul was shown) takes place, the woman is left with one final and crucial step in the meal's preparation, which we'll come back to. Let's first take a closer look at the woman in the parable.

The Woman Preparing the Meal: The woman preparing the three measures of bread dough is one and the same with:

* The Woman whom God the Father is speaking of in the Book of Genesis 3:15 when He says to the serpent: *"I will put enmity between thee and 'the woman,' and thy seed and her seed: she shall crush thy head, and thou shalt lie in wait for her heel..."*
* The Woman who gave birth to Jesus' first coming.
* The Woman Elizabeth called "blessed among all woman" and referred to as *"the mother of my Lord."* (Luke 1:42-43)
* The Woman at the wedding feast of Cana to whom Jesus said: *"Woman, what is that to me and to thee?"* (John 2:3-4)
* The Woman to whom Jesus spoke these words from the cross: *Woman, behold thy Son,* as He gave His beloved disciple John to her as a son – see John 19-26-7.
* The Woman his beloved disciple John in the Book of Revelation, chapter 12, would subsequently refer to seven times, *once as "**a woman**"—the other six times as "**the woman**.*" (The chapter begins: *"And a great sign appeared in heaven, a woman clothed with the sun, and the moon under her feet, and on her head a crown of twelve stars: And being with child, she cried travailing in birth, and was in pain to be delivered."* (Revelation 12:1-2)

Thus the Woman preparing the three measures of meal—the Marriage Supper of the Lamb—is none other than the Most Blessed Virgin Mary—the Mother of God.

Therefore, the pregnant woman St. John is referring to in Revelation Chapter 12, as travailing in pain and about to give birth, is the same woman who gave birth to Jesus—the Risen Bread of Life. <u>This is because in the same way the Virgin Mary gave birth to Jesus' First Coming, so too is She now laboring in pain and about to give birth to His Second Coming—Jesus within us—the revelation/unveiling of the sons of God—the unveiling of the bread dough</u>! The birthing process is taking place through her authentic apparitions and private revelations throughout the world, especially through the writings of the Servant of God Luisa Piccarreta[49].

(Jesus' Third and final coming takes place in the clouds as evidenced in Matthew 24:30 and Luke 21:27.)

The Hidden Leaven: The understanding that the three measures of bread dough are a metaphor for the Blessed Trinity is necessary to comprehend this profound parable's teaching. However, in order to comprehend the full meaning of this parable it is necessary to grasp that Jesus is not likening the Kingdom of Heaven to the meal of bread but to the "leaven," which is the ingredient that causes bread dough to rise into wholeness. Note how Jesus says, *"the Kingdom of Heaven is like unto leaven!"*

---

49 Through the knowledge given to Luisa Piccarreta by God in 36 volumes called <u>Book of Heaven</u>, Our Father's Name will be hallowed and His Kingdom will come and His "Divine Will" will be done on earth as it is in Heaven. **The saints have done God's Will – the knowledge given to Luisa imparts to us not only how "to do" God's Divine Will but how to come to "live in" His Divine Will – there's literally a world of difference in doing His Will and coming to live in His Divine Will**. The author recommends going to the website www.queenoflight.org to learn more about this.

Therefore, the "key" to understanding this parable's crucial teaching lies in the "knowledge" of the hidden leaven—which Jesus tells us the woman has taken and "hidden" in the bread dough.

Of major importance is the parable's indication that the woman has <u>hidden the key to the knowledge</u> of the secret rising ingredient until the time when her meal—the Kingdom of Heaven—rises into wholeness.

<u>The "Key" to the Kingdom of Heaven's Rise into Wholeness is the "Knowledge" of the Hidden Leaven</u>: In the following verse Jesus chastises the lawyers for having taken away the key of knowledge to the Kingdom of Heaven: *"Woe to you lawyers for you have taken away **the key of knowledge,** you yourselves have not entered in [the Kingdom of Heaven], and those that were, you have hindered."* (Luke 11:52)

In Jesus' next words, recorded three verses later, He connects "the key of knowledge" with leaven: *"Beware ye of **the leaven** of the Pharisees, which is hypocrisy. For there is **nothing covered** that shall not be revealed, **nor hidden** that shall not be made known."* (Luke 12:1-2) Note in particular how Jesus connects the key of knowledge with leaven that has been covered and hidden. Here, Jesus is making us aware that because the Pharisees were not entering into the Kingdom of Heaven they took away its key—the knowledge of the good leaven—and replaced it with a leaven of hypocrisy.

Next Jesus indicates that in time the leaven of hypocrisy that has been *covered* will be revealed. Then, alluding to the good leaven, Jesus says that which has been *hidden* (by the woman in the bread dough) will be made known!

Dear brethren, the key to the knowledge of the secret leaven that has been hidden by the woman is now being made known because the meal she has been preparing—the Kingdom of Heaven—is about to rise into wholeness.

The Key of Knowledge: The powerful knowledge of the secret leaven—which will prove to be the substance salt—is the key that will bring about the rise of the Kingdom of Heaven within us into wholeness.

The knowledge of this key will help us to comprehend the great magnitude of this important question the Word of God poses to us in Sacred Scripture:

> *"Did you not know that the Lord God of Israel gave to David the Kingdom over Israel 'forever', to him and his sons, 'by a covenant of salt?"* (2 Chronicles/Paralipomenon 13:5)

Wow! If God gave David and his sons the Kingdom over Israel forever by a Covenant of Salt—would not the substance salt, which just so happens to be a leaven, be the key that opens the door to the knowledge of the mystery of God's Kingdom?

This would add a depth of insight into Colossians 4:3-6, where St Paul asks us to pray that a *"door of speech"* be opened to him *"to speak the Mystery of Christ."* Three verses later the door of speech is opened with his words: *"Let your speech be always in grace seasoned with 'salt' so that you may know how to answer every question."* The humble and simple substance salt will prove to be the key to speak the knowledge of the Mystery of Christ and His rise into fullness.

Dear brothers and sisters in Christ Jesus, what we will come to understand is that "the Old Salt Covenant Promise" God made with David, was a foreshadowing of "the New Salt Covenant Promise" that God is bringing into fulfillment through, with, and in the sanctifying substance salt found in the precious Body and Blood of Jesus Christ[50].

---

50 Without the substance salt our bodies could not live, move, or have being.

In fact, the salt in Jesus' Body and Blood will prove to be the better and more lasting substance of the promise—the promise God made with David and his sons—that St. Paul refers to in Hebrews 10:34-36 when he writes about the *"better"* and *"more lasting substance of the promise!"*

The following is one of many forthcoming examples from Sacred Scripture that shows the amazing healing power of the substance salt: Here Eliseus/Elisha—the great Old Testament prophet heals *"the spring of the waters"* of the Jordan from *"death or barrenness"* with *"a new vessel of salt: And the men of the city said to Eliseus: Behold the situation of this city is very good, as thou my Lord, seest: but the waters are very bad, and the ground barren. And he said: Bring me a <u>new vessel and put salt into it</u>. And when they had brought it, he went out to the spring of the waters, and cast the salt into it, and said: Thus saith the Lord: I have healed these waters, and there shall be no more in them death or barrenness. And the waters were healed unto this day, according to the word of Eliseus, which he spoke."* (4 (or 2) Kings 2:19-22)

Keeping in mind St. Paul's teaching that all scripture is meant for instruction, we are able to deduce from the above scripture that we—God's off-spring[51]—will also be healed from death and barrenness with a new vessel of salt. The new vessel is Jesus and the salt is the salt in His precious Body and Blood. (God's Salt Covenant is woven throughout this unveiling with particular emphasis in Chapter V.)

The key to the knowledge of God's Kingdom and its rising, within us, into wholeness will prove to be the catalyst that brings about the rising of the kingdom of evil—the bad leaven yeast—against it. Yeast, a fungus that lacks chlorophyll from the sun's light, will prove to be the bad leaven. It was of this day in time that Jesus was

---

51 In the Bible the children of God are often referred to as His "off-spring."

speaking when He foretold: *"For nation shall 'rise' against nation, and kingdom against kingdom..."* Matthew 24:7

The Meal's Preparation: Now let us return to the meal and review the steps the woman has taken in preparing it for us:

1) She has prepared three measures of bread dough in which she has put a secret leavening ingredient the knowledge of which is to remain hidden until the meal rises into wholeness.
2) Next she veils the bread dough.
3) Now she waits because it takes "time" for the meal—the Kingdom of Heaven— to rise into wholeness.

Wisdom! Let us be attentive! The parable then indicates that once the three measures of meal have risen into wholeness, as it is about to do, the woman is to reveal the secret rising ingredient, which she is now doing.

The Final Step in the Woman's Preparation of the Meal: The woman's final and crucial step in the preparation of the three measures of meal will be to unveil the risen bread dough and place it into the dome[52] shaped oven to be "fired." This step brings her meal to completion.

In order to enter into risen wholeness, the bread dough, like the Bread of Life, must pass through fire. Here it is good to ponder that it wasn't until Jesus revealed He was the Son of God that He was called a blasphemer, laughed at, spat on, persecuted, imprisoned, scourged, tortured by crucifixion and put to death. Thus, we can expect that when the revelation of the sons of God—our unveiling—takes place,

---

52 Ovens were dome shaped in Jesus' time. The dome oven symbolizes God's King-dome and its testing through fire.

we will have a part in the same sufferings Jesus underwent. It was precisely for this reason that Jesus said that, like Him, we would be persecuted, dragged before kings and governors, imprisoned, and some of us even put to death!

Be Not Afraid: Saint John Paul II often reminded us that we are not to fear. One good reason we are not to fear is that everything that happened to Jesus—including all the wonderful events[53]—will be repeated in us, His Mystical Body. This means that just as Jesus was strengthened by His transfiguration into Glory, which preceded His passion and death, so too will we be strengthened at the unveiling of the sons of God—our transfiguration into glory—the outward manifestation of Jesus' Glory within us. Then, just as Jesus' Heart was on fire with love for us, so too will our hearts be aflame with love for Him and one another—this coincides with the long awaited second Pentecost. And, just as Jesus longed to embrace the cross that would crown His Heavenly Father King of Glory, so too will we long to embrace the cross that crowns our Heavenly Father with all the Glory He is so deserving of. Everything must come full circle.

---

53 These wonderful things include the Mysteries of Light, which John Paul II the Great has given to us. These mysteries on the life of Jesus take place before His passion and death. Like Jesus, we too will walk through these magnificent Mysteries of Light—miracles and wonders will abound. We will experience this awesome day in the Lord, like Jesus, just before we enter into our hour of darkness—the Sorrowful Mysteries. The "Good News" is that for all eternity we will live out the Glorious Mysteries with the Lord, world without end. AMEN!

CHAPTER 3

§

*"And may the God of Peace himself sanctify you in all things,
that your whole spirit, and soul, and body, may be
preserved blameless in the coming of Jesus Christ."*

2 THESSALONIANS 4:23

The Number Three And the Divine Rising

A KEY ELEMENT IN THIS explanation on the Kingdom of Heaven's rise into wholeness is the number three, as seen in the three measures of meal.

Numbers are meaningful because *"God hast ordered all things in measure, and number, and weight."* (Wisdom 11:21) For example, the number three is known as the divine number because it symbolizes the three Divine Persons in one God—the Blessed Trinity.

In the parable on the Kingdom of Heaven's rise into wholeness found in Matthew 13:33, the number three also signifies "a rising," the rising of the "three measures" of bread dough into wholeness!

The number three's connection with a rising is further evidenced in the fact that Jesus rose from the dead on the third day. Also the New Covenant records three others as having been raised from the dead by Jesus: the widow's son, Jairus' daughter, and Lazarus.

GOD USES THE NATURAL TO REVEAL THE SUPERNATURAL

As creatures of the senses, we need the natural to make sense of God's supernatural plan. For this reason, the three basic ingredients used to unite flour into bread dough: water, salt, and oil, are the very three forms of matter used in Baptism—the Sacrament that unites us to Jesus—the Bread of Everlasting Life! (This is a good place to ponder on the Gospel of John 6:30-66 wherein Jesus repeatedly instructs us that He is the Bread of Life that we must partake of in order to have life everlasting.)

The Three Forms of Matter Used in the Sacrament of Baptism: These three forms of sacramental matter used in Baptism—water, salt[54] and oil—will be shown to be related to the three components of man's being: spirit, soul, and body!

Our Entrance into the Life of the three Divine Persons in one God: In addition, these three forms of sacramental matter are supernaturally inseparable from our entrance into the divine life of the three Divine Persons in one God—the Father, the Son and the Holy Spirit.

In the light of Scripture, as supported by science, the correspondence among the three Persons in One God; the three components of man's being; and the three forms of sacramental matter will be shown in the next chapters to be as follows:

1.) The First Person of the Blessed Trinity:	God the Father	Spirit	Water
2.) The Second Person of the Blessed Trinity:	God the Son	Soul	Salt
3.) The Third Person of the Blessed Trinity:	God the Holy Spirit	Body	Oil

So far, the three measures of meal represent:

---

54 Recall that the holy tradition of putting blessed and exorcised salt in the waters of Baptism has in recent times been made optional for Catholics of the Roman Rite.

- ❧ The three forms of matter used in the sacrament of Baptism—water, salt and oil.
- ❧ The three components of man: spirit, soul, and body.
- ❧ The three Persons in one God: Father, Son and Holy Spirit, comprising the Holy Trinity

The three Divine Persons in one God can be viewed through the lens of these three dimensions through which God reveals Himself to us in time and space!

The Sanctification of our *"whole Spirit, and Soul, and Body… in the Coming of Jesus Christ"*: In the parable of the bread dough, the rising of the three measures of meal into wholeness is a metaphor for the rising of the Kingdom of Heaven within us into wholeness! This wholeness, which represents our complete and perfect unity with the Whole Trinity, is providentially reflected in St. Paul's prayer for our sanctification: *"And may the God of Peace himself sanctify you in all things, that your whole spirit, and soul, and body, may be preserved blameless in the 'coming of Jesus Christ."* (2 Thessalonians 4:23)

Saint Paul was given over to praying these words because the woman who is preparing the three measures of meal, the Blessed Mother, hid the key to the knowledge of our rising into wholeness of spirit, soul and body, in his epistles.

The key which was hidden (by the Woman in the three measures of bread dough/us) and is now being made known is the knowledge of the sanctifying substance Salt found in the precious Body and Blood of Jesus Christ! This is the Salt of the New Covenant built on a better and more lasting substance of the promise. The knowledge of the leaven salt will prove necessary to bring about the rising of all things into fullness in Christ Jesus.

Dear sisters and brothers in Christ Jesus, in order for our sanctification *"in all things"* to take place, we must embrace the full knowledge of Our Lord and Savior Jesus Christ that is being un-veiled. God is ever so mercifully imparting this knowledge to us now because the fullness of time is approaching.

THE VIRGIN OF THE REVELATION

Saint Paul received His Revelations of the Lord in the Third Heaven where he heard Secret Words: We saw in 2 Corinthians 12:1-8 that St. Paul received his *"visions and revelations of the Lord"* (vs.1) while *"caught up to the third heaven"* (vs.2), where he was *"caught up into paradise, and heard secret words"* (vs.4). This is important to understand because:

1) The *"revelations of the Lord"* St. Paul received in the third Heaven will prove to correspond with the revelations of the three measures of meal the woman is now unveiling.
2) The *"secret words"* St. Paul heard in the third Heaven will prove to correspond with the secret rising ingredient the woman hid in the three measures of meal and is now revealing.

It is no coincidence that St. Paul received his revelations of the Lord in the "Third Heaven," once again, the number three points to a divine rising!

The Woman preparing the Three Measures of Meal appears in Three Fountains, Rome under the title "The Virgin of the Revelation": Previously we saw that the Woman, our Blessed Mother, who is preparing the three measures of bread dough, is the same Woman of the Book of Revelation Chapter 12, who is with child, laboring to give birth. We also noted that her painful birthing process is taking place through her travails, as in apparitions, throughout the world. With this in mind, one apparition site of major significance when it comes to Her birthing of the sons of God, the unveiling of Christ Jesus within us, is the site where she appeared on April 12, 1947, under the very title "The Virgin of the Revelation" in the square of "Tre Fontane", Rome, Italy. (Tre Fontane is translated "Three Fountains"—noting yet again the number three's connection with this powerful unveiling of Sacred Scripture!)

Interestingly enough, this apparition, which is recognized and beautifully commemorated by the Church, took place across the street from the sacred ground where St. Paul was martyred by decapitation—whereupon his head bounced "three times", and "three fountains" miraculously rose up. These three springs, which over time have become polluted, still exist. (On a universal scale, these three now polluted springs are representative of the pollution that has taken place in the world, the flesh, and the spirit.)

The following is a little history of what took place in the grotto of the Three Fountains: On April 12, 1947, Our Lady appeared to a man named Bruno Cornacchiola and his three children. At the time, Bruno, a trolley conductor, had an intense hatred for the Catholic Church and the Virgin Mary—especially towards the Church's dogma of the Immaculate Conception. In fact, as his children played ball in the grotto he was plotting to kill the Holy Father on the feast of Our Lady's birthday – September 8th.

Our Lady first appeared to Bruno's three young children before appearing to him. Bruno however was the only one to hear her speak. At the onset of the heavenly visitation, Bruno explains "I suddenly saw two pure white hands moving towards me and I felt they were lightly touching my face. I felt the sensation that something was being pulled from my eyes."[55] This is reminiscent of the scales that were removed from St. Paul's eyes. Bruno was then uplifted from the earth and brought to the brightest point where he was given the vision of a beautiful woman in radiant light "She was wearing a brilliant white tunic, gathered at the waist with a pink sash, the two ends of which reached her knees. Her hair was black, pulled back to her head. Some of it showed under the green veil that covered her from head to foot, like a beautiful royal mantle."[56] Bruno explained that these colors have a connection with Our Lady's relationship to the Three Divine Persons. This is illustrated in the following excerpts taken from Monsignor Fausto Rossi's book The Virgin of the Revelation, pages 49-50:

"The GREEN STANDS FOR THE FATHER, i.e. it represents creation as synthesized in Mother Earth. In the book of Genesis we read how God the Father created all things."

"The WHITE IS THE SON. 'In the beginning was the word: the word was with God and the word was God. He was with God in the beginning. Through Him all things came to be, not one thing had its being but through him."

"The PINK (symbolizing love) is the HOLY SPIRIT. 'For her co-operation with the Spirit, the Virgin is the Mother of Our Lord, the Messiah, and is the origin of the community of the New Covenant. She symbolizes the Church, Virgin and Mother, who generates God's children in the Spirit."

---

55 Msgr. Fausto Rossi, The Virgin of the Revelation pg. 13

56 Msgr. Fausto Rossi, The Virgin of the Revelation pg. 14

The Virgin of Revelation identified herself as "Daughter of the Father, the Mother of the Son, and Spouse and Temple of the Holy Spirit." She then revealed to Bruno that these colors also have a connection with the three apparitions of Fatima, Lourdes and Rome.

These are the words she spoke first to Bruno "I am She who is with the Holy Trinity. I am the VIRGIN OF THE REVELATION. You persecuted me, enough now. Enter into the heavenly fold, which is the heavenly court on earth."[57] The Virgin of the Revelation then talked at length to Bruno catechizing him and also giving him instruction for the faithful. She emphasized "Always pray and recite the rosary daily for the conversion of sinners and non-believers and for Christian unity. The Hail Mary's that you say with faith and love are as many golden arrows that pierce the heart of Jesus."[58]

Emphasizing the mystery of her intimacy with the Holy Trinity the Virgin revealed "My body could not perish and did not perish. My Son and the angels came to claim me at the moment of my death." (Approximately three and a half years later on November 1, 1950, Pope Pius XII proclaimed the dogma of the Assumption of the Blessed Virgin Mary into Heaven)

At one point during the apparition Our Lady, The Virgin Mary, who was holding a closed small grey book, clutched to her breast with both hands, removed her left hand and pointed down towards her feet to a torn black cloth on which Bruno saw a broken cross. Bruno was given over to believe that the black cloth represented clerical vestments and other distinguishing signs that many religious people have discarded.

---

57 The Virgin of the Revelation pg. 15
58 The Virgin of the Revelation, pg. 17

The Virgin of the Revelation entrusted Bruno with the following message for priests, as illustrated by Monsignor Fausto Rossi in his book <u>The Virgin of the Revelation</u> on pg. 93:

"TO DEEPER FAITH IN THE REVEALED TRUTHS.
(which means certainty of a reward and of eternal punishments.)

TO GREATER OBEDIENCE TO THE TEACHING OF THE CHURCH.
(in prayer, in liturgical celebrations, in the way of dressing.)

TO VIGILANT PRUDENCE WHEN DEALING WITH PEOPLE.
(in the distribution of the Sacraments and in daily relations.)
Furthermore, **TO A PURE AND DIGNIFIED STYLE OF LIFE."**

Like at Fatima and Lourdes, the Virgin of the Revelation speaks of the need of our prayers —in particular the Holy Rosary for the conversion of sinners and unbelievers. As at Fatima,[59] a mystery surrounds a secret message that the Virgin of the Revelation gave to the visionary for the Pope. It is plausible that the revelation of this secret message is taking place now in this amazing unveiling of Sacred Scripture.

By the way, a beautiful Order of Sisters named, "The Missionaries of Divine Revelation" were founded to honor Our Lady's apparitions at this site in Three Fountains, Rome. Their attractive "olive green" habits are the color of the mantle the Virgin of the Revelation wore during the visitation.

There is also another beautiful Order of Sisters founded by St. Lucy Filippini in 1692 called "The Religious Teachers Filippini.'" Many of these wonderful Sisters have promulgated devotion to the Virgin of the Revelation. Their devotion began when Bruno, the visionary, was instructed by the Virgin of Revelation to go to these "Pious Sisters" and ask them to pray for all non-believers and sinners. This pious Order of Sisters has provinces in many countries throughout the world, with two in the USA.

In 1997 the apparition site of "The Virgin of the Revelation" was named by the Pope, now Saint John Paul II, <u>Holy Mary of the Third Millennium at Three Fountains</u>.

The Hidden Mystery "Now" Being Manifested: Dear saints, St. Paul is referring to the hidden Mystery of Christ that the Virgin of the Revelation is now revealing when he writes, *"**The mystery** which has been **hidden** from ages and generations but is **now being manifested to the saints...**"* This mystery is *"now"* being manifested to the saints because the Kingdom of Heaven—which Jesus in Matthew 13:33 likens to the Three Measures of Meal the Woman is preparing—is about to rise into wholeness.

---

59 The 100th year anniversary of Our Lady of Fatima's apparitions will take place May 13, 2017 through October 13, 2017. Eventful times in world history is anticipated.

How do we know the Kingdom is about to rise into wholeness? Because the woman of the parable—the Virgin of the Revelation—is now revealing the knowledge of the secret rising ingredient she hid in the meal. In the light of the parable, this signifies that the unveiling of the bread dough, synonymous with the revelation of the sons of God, is about to take place.

There are no coincidences, so please don't miss the subtle, but simple, correlations in the above. These numerous connections are not only with the number three but also with the word revelation, synonymous with unveiling, as seen in the following:

1. "*The **revelations** of the Lord*" that St. Paul was shown.
2. "The Woman of the Book of **Revelation**" Chapter 12.
3. The apparition of "The Virgin of the **Revelation.**"
4. "*The **revelation** of the sons of God.*"
5. "*The **revelation** of the mystery kept secret from eternity.*" (Recall that this was the theme of the previous chapter which emphasized St. Paul's gospel having to do with the unveiling of hidden knowledge, "*Now to him that is able to establish you, according to my gospel, and the preaching of Jesus Christ, according to 'the revelation of the mystery' which was kept secret from eternity.*" (Romans 16:25)

<u>The Virgin of the Revelation's unique Mission</u>: Everywhere Our Lady appears she does so under a unique title that reflects her special mission at the particular apparition site. For instance, under the title "The Virgin of the Revelation" the Blessed Mother's mission would naturally have to do with a revelation—an unveiling.

Her appearance under this title in close proximity to St. Paul's Church in Rome indicates that her mission would likely correspond to St. Paul's gospel and the preaching of Jesus Christ according to *"the revelation of the mystery,"* an unveiling of hidden knowledge, he was given. St. Paul instructs us that this unveiling of the mystery, which was kept secret from eternity, is now, in due time, being made known to the saints!

On the day of this apparition the Virgin of the Revelation asked the people specifically to pray for Christian unity. This request also uniquely corresponds with St. Paul's letters in which he writes that in order to enter into the unity of faith we need to be given the full knowledge of the Son of God, the unveiling of the secret knowledge, which is now being revealed. *"For the perfecting of the saints, for the work of the ministry, for the edifying of the body of Christ; Until we all meet into the unity of faith, and of the knowledge of the Son of God, unto a perfect man, unto the <u>measure</u> of the age of <u>the fullness of Christ</u>."*

Wisdom! Be attentive: The *"measure"* of the age of *"the fullness of Christ"* St. Paul is referring to parallels Jesus' parable of the three <u>measures</u> of meal that are now rising into <u>fullness</u>. They are now rising into unity and fullness through the knowledge of salt, the secret leavening ingredient the woman hid in the three measures and is now manifesting to the saints.

<u>The Knowledge of the secret/hidden leaven is the Key that opens the Door to the Preaching the Mystery of Christ, the Revelation of the Mystery kept Secret from all eternity!</u> Recall how St. Paul in Colossians 4:3-6 invokes our prayers that *"a door of speech to speak the Mystery of Christ"* be open to him and to his disciples *"to preach the Mystery of Christ."* Then three verses later he instructs us: *"Let your speech be always in grace **sea**soned with **salt** that you may know how you ought to answer every man."* Since to know how to answer every man we are to season our speech with the "leaven" salt, salt will prove to be the key that opens the door of speech to preach the Mystery of Christ and His rise into fullness.

In addition, since salt is also a preservative that frees things from corruption and St. Paul in I Corinthians 15:53 instructs us that our *"corruptible body"* must put on *"incorruption,"* would salt then point to the key to our incorruption—the very *"Key of Knowledge"* to the Kingdom of Heaven Jesus accused the Pharisees of taking from the people?

Also, since Eliseus healed the spring of the waters of the Jordan from death and barrenness with a vessel of salt, would not salt be the healing remedy that will set the three polluted springs in Tre Fontane, Rome, free from pollution?

Moreover, if salt is indeed the key of knowledge to the Kingdom of Heaven and its rise within us into wholeness, wouldn't salt be the key that opens and shuts the door to the Kingdom of Heaven, the very —*"Key of David"*— to which Isaiah 22:22 and Revelation 3:7 refer?

> *"And I will lay the key of the house of David upon his shoulder: and he shall open, and none shall shut: and he shall shut, and none shall open."* (Isaias 22:22)

> *"And to the angel of the church of Philadelphia, write: These things saith the Holy One and the true one, he that hath the key of David; he that openeth, and no man shutteth; shutteth, and no man openeth."* (Rev. 3:7)

Dear friends in Christ Jesus, God promised David and his sons the Kingdom over Israel forever by a Covenant of Salt – did He not?

And did not Jesus in Mark 9:49 state: *"Have salt in you and have peace among you?"*

The answer to these important and meaningful questions will be demonstrated with clarity throughout this powerful unveiling of Sacred Scripture.

The Third Heaven and Earth: Of corresponding significance, St. Peter, who like St. Paul was martyred in Rome, instructs us that the first heaven and earth was destroyed by water and that the second heaven and earth—in which we now live—is reserved unto fire as seen in II Peter 3:6-12. St. Peter follows this up by stating, *"But we look for new heavens and a new earth according to 'his promises,' in which justice dwelleth."* (II Peter 3:13)

Since the second heaven and earth in which we now live is reserved unto fire, this indicates that before we can enter the New Heaven and Earth, which would be the Third Heaven and Earth, we, like the bread dough, must pass through the *"fire"* of the second heaven and earth—into risen wholeness or fullness.

Jesus was speaking of the second Heaven and earth and the fire we must pass through when He said: *"For every one shall be <u>salted with fire</u>: and every victim shall be <u>salted with salt."</u>* (Mark 9:48)

<u>The Rising of "all things" into Universal Holiness in the Third Heaven and Earth:</u> Another level of meaning the knowledge of the three measures of meal will take on in this unveiling of Sacred Scripture is their representation of the rising of all things: 1) of the spirit, 2) of the flesh 3) and of the world—into universal wholeness or holiness.

This makes sense because Jesus is the risen Bread of Life in whom all fullness dwells. St. Paul puts it this way, *"Because in him it hath well pleased the Father, that all fullness should dwell; And through Him to reconcile 'all things' unto Himself, making peace through the blood of His cross, both as to the things that are 'on earth', and the things that are in 'heaven."* (Colossians 1:19)

The Gospel of the Glory of Christ's rise into fullness now being unveiled is the full knowledge of our Lord and Savior Jesus Christ that Father Mary Joachim prophesied is needed to set us free from the defilement of this world. In his booklet "The Mystery of the

Second Coming," Fr. Joachim writes, "How does one escape the de-filement of the world? As the gravest effect of the sin of Adam and Eve is the spiritual blindness of which we are all subject, the great grace we need is the enlightenment and 'the full knowledge of the Lord and Savior Jesus Christ.' This comes only with the unfolding of the mystery of the Epiphania, when the Gospel of the Glory of the Blessed God is proclaimed."

This wondrous knowledge of the rising of Christ's Kingdom of Glory into fullness and how this rising is taking place within us—Christ's Mystical Body—is St. Paul's Gospel of the Glory of Christ now being unveiled. The preaching of this astonishing knowledge of how the Son of God—through the Blood of His Cross—has emp-tied Himself into us, making us sons of God, co-heirs, is the full knowledge of the Son of God that is necessary to bring about the unity of faith, the new era of peace and the perfect glorification of the Holy Trinity. Of this age of universal holiness we call to mind again St. Paul words: *"Until we all meet unto the unity of faith, and of the knowledge[60] of the Son of God', unto a perfect man."* (Ephesians 4:13)

To recapitulate: So far we have seen the link between the num-ber three and the rising of all things, in Heaven and on earth, into universal fullness/holiness nine times:

1. The three measures of meal
2. The three Comings of Christ
3. The three elements of sacramental matter
4. The three Persons in one God

---

60 Throughout his letters Saint Paul instructs us to increase in the knowledge of God, i. e. in Philippians 1:9 he writes, *And this I pray, that your charity may more and more abound in knowledge, and in all understanding; That you may approve the better things, that you may be sincere without offence unto the day of Christ.* Then in Colossians 2:2, *That their hearts may be comforted, being instructed in charity, and unto all riches of fullness of understanding, unto the knowledge of the mystery of God the Father and of Christ Jesus, in whom are 'hid' all the treasures of wisdom and knowledge.*

5. The three components of man
6. The three dimensions of God, as pertains to time and space
7. The three heavens and earth
8. The three times St. Paul's head bounced when decapitated, whereat three fountains arose.
9. The rising of all of the world, the flesh, and the spirit into universal wholeness

Three times three is nine; nine being the number of the fruits of the Holy Spirit. These fruits of the spirit are listed by St. Paul in 1 Corinthians 12:8-10, *"To one indeed, by the Spirit, is given the word of wisdom, and to another, the word of knowledge, according to the same Spirit; To another, faith in the same spirit; to another, the grace of healing in one Spirit; to another, the working of miracles; to another, prophecy; to another, the discerning of spirits; to another, diverse kinds of tongues; to another, interpretation of speeches.."*

Nine also happens to be the number of divine completion because it was at the *ninth hour*[61] that God's plan of salvation was brought into completion. At this hour, 3PM, Our Lord and Savior Jesus Christ died on the cross. His last Words were, *"It is consummated"* (also translated *"It is completed"*).

Dear sisters and brothers in Christ Jesus, the next five chapters will present the transformative knowledge of the Son of God's life-giving Water, sanctifying Salt, and unction of Olive Oil. God is now making known this striking gift of knowledge because it is necessary to: a) heal our fallen and wounded nature; b) restore us back to His image and likeness, and; c) bring about the complete restoration of all things in Heaven and on earth.

(Bear in mind that the Gospels of Matthew, and Mark, and Luke and John proclaim the life and Glory of the Son of God—Our

---

61 Matthew 27:45

Lord and Savior Jesus Christ, whereas St. Paul's gospel, which was hidden and is only now in the last time being unveiled, is about the life and Glory of the sons of God—within whom Christ Jesus is now rising into fullness.)

The chapters will cover:

1.) The invisibility of "God the Father," as corresponds to "the Spirit and Water."
2.) The visibility of "God the Son," as corresponds to "the Soul and Salt."
3.) The glorious luminosity of "God the Holy Spirit," as corresponds to "the Body and Oil."

As you read and contemplate the Revelation of the Mystery of Christ's Glory being made known, note the three means used to unveil it:

1.) **The Bible**, using the interpretative methods of:
   a) Scripture interpreting Scripture
   b) The literal meaning of Scripture.
2.) **The Catechism of the Catholic Church**.
3.) **Science**—simple enough for a child to understand.

CHAPTER 4

"But the water that I will give him,
shall become in him a fountain of water,
springing up into life everlasting."

(JOHN 4:14)

God the Father: Invisible - Spirit - Water

§

THE CATHOLIC CHURCH TEACHES THAT we enter into the Mystical Body of Christ through the Sacrament of Baptism. Providentially, one of the three forms of matter used in Baptism is water—the primary element of God's Glory. With this in mind we are now going to take a brief, but crucial, look at how God uses water to mystically represent the First Person of the Holy Trinity—God the Father.

GOD THE FATHER—AN INVISIBLE SPIRIT

It is a teaching of the Church that God the Father, the first Person of the Holy Trinity, is a Spirit. The Church also teaches that you cannot see a spirit. Therefore God the Father is an invisible Spirit.

In his letter to the Colossians 1:15, St. Paul makes reference to God the Father's invisibility in relationship to His Son Jesus, who gives Him visibility: *"Who [Jesus] is the image of the invisible God, the fullness of all creation."*

The Fountain of Living Water: In the Book of Jeremiah 2:13, God the Father mystically reveals Himself as the Fountain of Living Water: *"For my people have done two evils. They have forsaken me, the*

Fountain of Living Water, and have dug cisterns, that can hold no water." See also Jeremiah 17:13.

Jesus was speaking of the Fountain of Living Water when He encountered the Samaritan woman at Jacob's well, saying to her, *"Whosoever drinketh of this water, shall thirst again; but he that shall drink of the water that I will give him, shall become in him a fountain of water, springing up into life everlasting."* (John 4:13-14) We will return to the important distinction between the water at Jacob's well and the water from God the Father, the Fountain of Life Everlasting.

Our Baptism in God the Father's life-giving water is so vital that Jesus said to Nicodemus, *"Amen, Amen I say to thee, that unless a man be 'born again of water' and the Holy Ghost, he cannot enter into the Kingdom of God. That which is born of the flesh, is flesh, and that which is 'born of the spirit' is spirit."* (John 3:5-6) Note how Jesus equates being born of water with being born of the Spirit.

Now listen attentively to these admonishing words of St. Peter in which he speaks out against what he calls *"deceitful scoffers,"* whom he says will appear *"in the last days,"* denying this powerful knowledge of God's life-giving water: *"For this they are willfully ignorant of, that the heavens were before, and the earth out of water, and through water, 'consisting of the word of God."* (2 Peter 3:4-5) (Also consider how in the Book of Revelations 1:15 the voice of God, as in Word of God, is described as *"the sound of many waters!"*)

One reason St. Peter warns us that we must not be ignorant that the heavens were before, and the earth out of water, and through water, consisting of the Word of God, is because the knowledge of God's life-giving Water that is now, in the last time, being un-veiled represents the powerful weapon that will conquer and chain the enemy (Satan and his cohorts) and bring God's plan of salvation into completion. St. Peter also wanted to warn against the deceptive evolutionary philosophies of our day, which deny that God created the heavens and the earth and all they contain by His Fiat in the beginning.

The Invisibility of Water: Perhaps you are wondering: If God the Father is a spirit and a spirit has no visibility, how can water, which has visibility, represent Him? The answer is simple, please take a few seconds and wave your hand through the air about you—there is water in this air. You cannot see this water because it is in the form of water vapor. In fact, meteorologists are even able to measure this invisible water—it is called specific humidity.

Heaven's Life-Giving Water as Opposed to the Earth's Water: Since we saw in the above how the Word of God is likened to water, you might then ask: Why did Jesus when speaking to the Samaritan woman at Jacob's well, differentiate the water she was drawing from the well with God's everlasting water?

The answer is that the purity of Heaven's life-giving Water is separated from the impurity of the earth's water by a dome. This is seen in Genesis 1:6-7, *"And God said: Let there be a firmament [dome] made amidst the waters; and let it divide the waters from the waters. And God made a firmament [dome], and divided the waters that were under the firmament [dome], from those that were above the firmament [dome], and it was so."*

Next you might ask: How then is Jesus able to bring Heaven's life-giving Water to earth for the woman at the well to partake of?

The answer to this question lies in <u>"the power of His spoken Word."</u>

This power is most evident at the Consecration of the Mass, whereby bread and wine are changed (transubstantiated) into the very Body and Blood of Christ by the spoken words of <u>a Catholic Priest—Alter Christus—another Christ!</u>

Here, however, we are going to show the power in the extraordinary words of exorcism traditionally spoken by priests in the Roman Rite of the Catholic Church when praying over water to be used for Baptism as well as other blessings, i.e. of churches, of homes, and other places and objects.

The (+) symbol indicates where the priest makes the Sign of the Cross over the water while pronouncing these transformative words:

"O water, creature of God, I exorcise you in the Name of God the Father (+) Almighty, and in the Name of Jesus (+) Christ His Son, our Lord, and in the power of the Holy (+) Ghost. **I exorcise you so that you may put to flight all the power of the enemy**, and be able to root out and supplant that enemy with his apostate angels, through the power of our Lord Jesus Christ, who will come to judge the living and the dead and the world by fire. Amen"

"O God, for the salvation of mankind, You built your greatest mysteries on this substance, water. In your kindness, hear our prayers and pour down the power of your blessing (+) into this element, made ready for many kinds of purifications. May this, your creature, become an agent of divine grace in the service of your mysteries, to drive away evil spirits and dispel sickness, so that everything in the homes and other buildings of the faithful that is sprinkled with this water, may be rid of all uncleanness and freed form every harm. Let no breath of infection and no disease-bearing air remain in these places. May the wiles of the lurking enemy prove of no avail. Let whatever might menace the safety and peace of those who live here be put to flight by the sprinkling of this water, so that the health obtained by calling upon your holy name may be made secure against all attacks. Through Christ our Lord. Amen." (Bold added)

If we could see, as did my pastor, the power blessed and exorcised Holy Water has over evil, we would use it daily to bless ourselves, our families, and our homes.

<u>We are made in the image and likeness of God</u>: Since we are made in the "image" and likeness of God Our Father who calls Himself the Fountain of Living Water, it is logical that our natural bodies would consist of water. Science also validates this with evidence showing that we are anywhere from fifty-five to seventy-five per cent water.

Consider the mountains of mystical knowledge revealed in the following biblical verses in which God is speaking to Job: *"Who shut up the sea with doors, when it broke forth as issuing out of the womb. When I made a 'cloud' the garment thereof, and wrapped it in a mist as in 'swaddling bands?' I set my bounds around it, and made it bars and 'doors.'"* (Job 38:8-10) In this same chapter, verses 28 & 29, we read: *"Who is the father of the rain? Or who begot the drops of dew? Out of whose 'womb' came the ice; and the frost from heaven who hath 'gendered' it?"* (Job 38:28-29) God did indeed build His greatest mysteries on the substance water!

Reflecting on the above verses, it's apparent that the *"cloud"* God is referring to is the Cloud of His Glory. The very Cloud that overshadowed the Immaculate Virgin Mary – through whose *"womb"* Jesus was conceived! Jesus, who, when born was wrapped in *"swaddling bands!"* Also note that the sea, God's Kingdom of Glory, is shut up with doors. These are the doors to which Jesus gave Peter the Keys. (Peter, a fisherman of the sea, water and salt, is again another example of how God uses the natural to reveal the supernatural.)

Yet, the most fascinating aspect of the above verses is that the water from Heaven—in the form of rain, dew, ice and frost—has been *"gendered!"* Amazing, is it not?

The following compelling depiction of God's Divinity being as crystalline fountains, was revealed to the Venerable Abyss Mary of Agreda: "Thus the conduits, which let the crystalline fountains of the Divinity from the eternal throne, meet first in the humanity of the Word and immediately thereafter in his holy Mother." As pertains to the dispersing of these waters to other creatures, the Abyss was given the following knowledge: "Neither had the fountains of waters as yet sprung out. The images and ideals of creatures had not yet broken forth from the fountains through the channels of God's goodness and mercy." She next writes, "In respect to the entire rest of the universe[62], these waters and fountains were still repressed and detained within the bound of the immense ocean of the Divinity; in His own Being there were as yet founts or currents for outward manifestation." [63]

Dear friends, you are now able to understand how God uses water—invisible everywhere about you—to represent God Our Father, the Fountain of Living Water, who likewise is invisible everywhere about you!

In the above, the teaching of the Church, Sacred Scripture, and Science have been used to show that the first Person of the Blessed Trinity—God the Father—is the Fountain of Living Water, an invisible Spirit who is everywhere.

---

62 Water, like God, fills all things in Heaven and on earth, i.e. animal, plant, rock, etc. Listen to this insight from Saint Augustine that came to him as he reflected on the food of his infancy: "For neither my mother nor my nurses stored their milk on breasts for me; but Thou didst bestow the food of my infancy through them, according to Thine ordinance, whereby 'Thou distribute Thy riches through 'the hidden springs of all things!'" Underline added

63 The Mystical City of God, Vol. 1 The Conception, pgs 66-67.

(It must not be misconstrued to say that God is water or water is God. Water is a substance of nature, an agent of divine grace that God uses as a sign of His supernatural spirit and powers.)

CHAPTER 5

*"Let your speech be always in grace
seasoned with salt, so that you may
know how you ought to answer every man."*

Colossians 4:6

God the Son: Visible - Soul - Salt

WE ARE NOW GOING TO see how salt mystically represents the second Person of the Holy Trinity—God the Son.

GOD USES THE VISIBLE THINGS OF THE WORLD TO REVEAL THE INVISIBLE

As you ponder this illuminating knowledge keep in mind how God uses the visible things of this world to help us clearly see His invisible power and divinity. As previously seen reflected in St. Paul's words, *"For the invisible things of Him, from the creation of the world, are clearly seen, being understood by the things which are made; His eternal power also, and divinity; so that they are inexcusable."* (Romans 1:20)

Salt Gives Pure Water Visibility: Chapter IV explained water's invisible state. The following is a simplified explanation on how salt gives "pure" water visibility.

Salt water covers approximately 70% of the earth's surface in the form of oceans, seas, gulfs and straits. The action of wind over the salt water blows the salt into the atmosphere, whereas the heat of the sun evaporates the water into the atmosphere in the form of invisible water vapor.

Next, when certain weather conditions prevail in the atmosphere, the invisible water vapor starts clinging to the salt—now termed salt nuclei—forming cloud droplets. When the accumulation of the "invisible water vapor" on the "salt nuclei" gets heavy enough it falls from the clouds to the earth as rain, mist, snow, sleet or hail.

The water eventually returns to the oceans by way of gravity. This process, which is always repeating itself, is known as the water cycle.

With the above water cycle in mind we are going to clearly see how water's visible process unveils God's invisible plan to restore universal holiness. First however we are going to look at how in the same way water receives its visibility from salt, so too does God the Fountain of Living Water, show forth His visibility mystically through salt.

By the way, you should know that although salt is the most prevalent form of condensation nuclei, there are other nuclei that also form water droplets, albeit impure ones, i.e. volcanic ash, dust, and air pollutants. Thus, in the same way salt, a white crystal, gives "pure clouds" their visibility, so too do air pollutants give dark, or "black clouds" their visibility.

Now that you know how salt gives "pure" clouds, rain, mist, snow, sleet, and hail, visibility the following will show how salt mystically gives God visibility.

God Made Visible: After being assured that she had found grace with God, the Immaculate Virgin Mary learned from the Archangel

Gabriel[64] that she was to conceive the Son of the Most High, where-upon Mary asked Gabriel how she was to conceive because she knew not man. The Archangel answered: *"The Holy Ghost shall come upon thee, and the power of the most high shall 'overshadow' thee and therefore also the Holy which shall be born of thee shall be called the Son of God."* (Luke 1:35)

Please think about this: God's Glory appeared throughout the Old Covenant in a cloud – a cloud which casts a shadow. Therefore, as will be further validated, it was the Cloud of God's Glory—the Shekinah—that overshadowed Mary. Thus, it was through the figure of a cloud, consisting of the purest water and salt, that Jesus was conceived—the perfect image of the invisible God.

So you see dearly beloved, the treasure of grace the Lord deposited in Mary and of which she continues to be full of, is symbolized by His life giving Water and sanctifying Salt that forms the Cloud of His Glory!

In a somewhat similar way, the Cloud of God's Glory overshadows us in the water and salt of our Baptism. It is no coincidence that water cleanses and salt is a preservative that literally cures and restores.

God the Father clothes the Sea – Jesus – in a Cloud and wraps Him in a Mist, as in swaddling Bands: Shrouded in mystery now being unveiled, the Old Covenant foretells Jesus' incarnation

---

64 ***In the original translations of the Bible Gabriel's greeting is called a "salutation." This is quite fascinating because the prefix "sal" means "more at salt!" Perhaps it's just coincidental that if you take the letter "u" out of the word salutation you get **saltation!** Another coincidence, if there is such a thing, is that the word saltation, which can be found in older versions of the Webster dictionary, is defined as a "leaping," recollecting how John the Baptist leapt in his mother's womb when Mary sal-uted (salted) Elizabeth, John's mother. In addition, a synonym given for the word salutation is **mutation** which is defined as **a change in hereditary material.** This is also fascinating because it suggests that it was due to Mary's saltation that Elizabeth was filled with the Holy Ghost! And, Elizabeth could have only been filled with the Holy Ghost if she was set free from both actual and the original sin **inherited** from Adam and Eve. St. Luke writes: *And it came to pass that when Elizabeth heard the salutation of Mary, the infant leaped in her womb. And Elizabeth was filled with the Holy Ghost.* (Luke 1:41)

through the symbolism of the "sea" clothed in a "cloud" issuing out of "the womb."

> *"Who shut up the sea with doors, when 'it' broke forth as issuing out of the womb? When I made a cloud the garment thereof, and wrapped **it** in a mist as in swaddling bands? I set my bounds around **it**, and made **it***[65] *bars and doors."* (Job 38:8-9)

First, note how this amazing verse corresponds with St. Luke's description of the Virgin birth of Jesus, *"And she brought forth [from her womb] her firstborn son, and clothed Him up in swaddling clothes..."* (Luke 2:7)

Secondly, note how the sea—representing the Kingdom of Heaven breaking forth from the womb, is clothed in a cloud—representing the Cloud of God's Glory!

Thirdly, note how the sea that issues forth from the womb is bound shut and barred with doors. This is incredible because it was to these doors, bound shut, to Heaven's sea of sanctifying salt and living waters, that Jesus gave Peter, a fisherman of the sea,[66] the Keys saying: *"And I will give to thee the keys of the Kingdom of Heaven. And whatsoever thou shalt bind upon earth, it shall be bound also in Heaven..."* (Matthew 16:19)

As we have seen, God also gave King David a key to His Kingdom, the salt key, the covenant of salt through which God promised David and his sons the Kingdom over Israel forever!

And it is to this Mystery of Christ's Glory—His Mystical Kingdom of sanctifying Salt and living Water—that St. Paul is also bound. Recall Colossians 4:3 wherein St. Paul asks us to pray that

---

65 *But God who is faithful, for our preaching which was to you, was not, It is, and It is not. For the Son of God, Jesus Christ who was preached among you by us, by me, and Sylvanus, and Timothy, was not, It is and It is not, but, It is, was in Him. For all the promises of God are in Him, It is: therefore also by him, amen to God unto our 'glory.'* (2 Cor. 1:18-20)

66 Peter who already had a natural affinity for salt and water, was now being drawn supernaturally to salt and water – Heaven's Sea – the visible revealing the invisible!

the Lord open to him, *"a door of speech to speak the mystery of Christ for which I am also bound."* Three verses later the prayer is answered when St. Paul opens the door of speech with these words, *"Let your speech be always in grace seasoned with salt that you may know how you ought to answer every man."*

The key that is now opening the door to speak the Mystery of Christ to which King David, St. Peter and St. Paul are bound is salt. Salt which just so happens to be a leaven!

Taking us back, once again, to the parable of the Kingdom of Heaven's rise into wholeness. Recall how the woman "hid" the knowledge (the key of knowledge) of the rising ingredient in the three measures of meal until the time when the meal rises into wholeness. The woman, the Virgin of the Revelation, is now revealing the hidden leaven, it is salt! She is now revealing the secret ingredient because the knowledge of salt is necessary to bring the rising of the meal she is preparing (the Kingdom of Heaven) into wholeness/holiness.

The Four Levels of Salt: Throughout this unveiling of salt's physical characteristics, note how salt's corresponding spiritual significance is always of greater magnitude. Also keep in mind the following four levels of salt, starting with the most profound:

1. The Salt in the Precious Blood of Jesus—dispensed to us through the seven sacraments. This salt gives everlasting life to our bodies and souls.
2. The blessed and exorcised salt[67] used by itself or in Holy Water. This powerful salt is used in Baptism, as well as to bless people, homes, churches, and other places and objects.

---

67 In Blessed Anne Catherine Emmerich's book, <u>The Life of Jesus Christ and Biblical Revelation</u>, she writes: "I was given to understand that the power to withdraw various regions of the earth from Satan's dominion by means of a blessing is signified by the words: 'Ye are the salt of the earth.' For the same reason is salt one of the ingredients of Holy Water." Vol. 1 pg. 21.

3. The ordinary/natural salt found in the earth and sea and for which there are thousands of uses, most notably table salt.
4. The salt Jesus refers to in Mark 9:49 as having lost its flavor. An example of this salt is Lot's wife who turned into a pillar of salt. Two other examples of salt that has lost its flavor are: a) What St. Jude refers to in verse 12 as *clouds without water.* b) What St. Peter refers to as *"fountains without water."* You see, if you take the water out of a cloud or fountain nothing would be left but salt which has lost its flavor.

SALT'S AMAZING POWER

The following will show how God uses the visible substance salt to make known the invisible glories of His Kingdom, *"His eternal power also, and divinity; so that they are inexcusable."* [68] As you read and contemplate this knowledge which reflects God's power and Divinity, envision St. Paul who is now instructing us from the Third Heaven.

Salt is essential to life: One good reason salt is essential to life is that it cleanses the blood. Without a sufficient amount of salt in the blood our bodies would become susceptible to infection and succumb to corruption[69] and death. In this same way the salt in the precious Body and Blood of Jesus, dispensed to us in the seven sacra-

68 Romans 1:20
69 Cystic Fibrosis is the number two child killer. A simple way to diagnose this disease in infants is to taste the child's skin—a "salty" taste tests positive. These children lose salt—the cleanser of bodily fluids. Some time ago the Cystic Fibrosis gene was linked to Jewish and German lineage. Could these children suffer as victim souls for the sins of their ancestors who have forsaken the Salt Covenant? Healing of the Ancestry prayers is always recommended! (Thanks to medical science, as well as prayer of course, many children diagnosed with CF are now living happy and productive lives. A cure is anticipated in the foreseeable future!)

ments, purifies our souls and sets us free from the corruption of sin. Without this Salt our souls would succumb to eternal death.

An interesting scientific study that testifies to salt's purifying properties on a universal scale comes from the results of a study conducted at Hebrew University in Jerusalem. In this study it was concluded, "The air that we breathe near the surface remains clean because of the fact that the oceans are salty."[70]

Another discovery that demonstrates how God uses the natural substance salt to reflect His supernatural plan of salvation is that scientists in drought-stricken areas are effectively spraying salt into the atmosphere from helicopters to seed rain. This is momentous because in the same way salt is successfully seeding rain into the atmosphere, so too will salt—the substance of Christ's Glory—seed the rain of Christ into the world, the very reign of Christ on earth!

This knowledge of salt's amazing abilities to set free from corruption, to purify, and to seed rain, is going to open Heaven's floodgates, saturating us with the Glory of God. To know Him is to love Him!

Salt's Ability to Produce Power: Another important role the substance salt plays in the body is that salt's two elements, sodium and chloride, are the major electrolytes[71] found in the blood. This means that, among other physiological functions, salt is essential in transmitting the body's muscle and nerve impulses, without which the body could not live, move, or have being. This corresponds spiritually in that without the salt in the Body and Blood of Jesus Christ we

---

70 <u>Journal of Science</u>, August 2002 issue.

71 An electrolyte is a mineral that carries an electrical charge when dispensed in a liquid, for example water or blood. Sodium & Chloride (salt) are the most abundant electrolytes in the blood accounting for approximately 77% of its electrical properties. Other electrolytes in the blood that make up the remaining 23% include calcium, magnesium, and potassium.

could not live, move, or have eternal being: *"For in Him we live, move, and have being."* (Acts 17:28)

It is also remarkable that salt initiates the first heart beat in a newly transplanted heart. It would then make sense that salt initiates the first beat of the human heart within a mother's womb at four weeks after conception. Thus it would correspond that the blessed and exorcised substance salt in the waters of Baptism initiates the first heart beat of our journey into everlasting life, our sacred unity with the Immaculate Heart of Mary and the Sacred Heart of Jesus.

A truly fascinating aspect of salt is its ability to produce light. For example, when salt is placed in a solution such as water it conducts an electrical current. This is due to salt's two elements sodium (+) and chloride (-), which disassociate into electrically charged particles—neutrons, protons, and electrons. As a matter of fact, oceanographers measure the amount of **sal**ine, as in salt, in the ocean by the "electrical conductivity" in the water.

A simple experiment that demonstrates the power in salt's electrical properties follows: If you take two electrodes and attach them to a flashlight bulb and battery and then place them into a beaker of water, nothing will happen. **However, when you put salt in the beaker of water the bulb will light up!** Supernaturally this is what takes place in our Baptism in blessed and exorcised salt and water. We become light—God's children of Light!

As the author was contemplating this knowledge of salt, you can imagine her delight when she read these words that our Blessed Mother spoke under the title "Our Lady of All Nations," **"The Holy Spirit of Peace is nearer now than ever before, but He will only come if you pray: He is the SALT, He is the WATER, He is the LIGHT!!!"** Caps added. This quotation was taken from the November 1998 issue of <u>Inside the Vatican.</u> (The apparition site of

Our Lady of All Nations is acknowledged by the Bishop of Haarlem, Amsterdam, Bishop Punt, to be of supernatural origin.)

Salt Signifies the Souls Sanctifying Substance we receive through God's Sea of Seven Sacraments: The attributes of salt's ability to produce power—light, heat, movement—as well as to purify, are magnified beyond our comprehension when it comes to the sanctifying power in the supernatural salt in the Body and Blood of Jesus Christ. This incredibly powerful salt from God's heavenly Sea of Glory, signifies the divine life that is poured into us in the seven sacraments. It is this sharing in God's life that makes us partakers of Jesus' Divine Nature. Through this sharing in the precious Body and Blood of Jesus we shall come *"to live as children of the light."* (Ephesians 5:8)

Some of the most magnificent mysteries of God's life-giving water and sanctifying salt have been revealed to the Servant of God Luisa Piccarreta. As seen, for example, in the book "<u>The Virgin Mary in the Kingdom of the Divine Will</u>" in which the Virgin Mary explains to Luisa how She was preserved from sin at Her conception: "And the Divinity, perceiving in me Its creative work beautiful and pure, smiled contentedly; and wanting to celebrate over me, **the Heavenly Father poured seas of Power upon me; the Son seas of Wisdom; the Holy Spirit seas of Love.** In this way I was conceived in the unending light of the Divine Will; and in the midst of **these divine seas**, which my littleness could not contain, I formed highest waves, sending them back as homage of love and Glory to the Father, to the Son, and to the Holy Spirit." (pg. 10) Another example is this excerpt from the Virgin Mary's description of Jesus at His resurrection, "He was all majesty, from His Divinity united to His soul sprang forth **seas of light**—and enchanting beauty so as to fill Heaven and earth." (Pg. 123, bold added)

This knowledge of the Son of God helps us to enter into a deeper understanding of Jesus' Sermon of the Mount in which He calls us *"the salt of the earth—the light of the world"* as seen in Matthew 5:13-14.

THE SALT COVENANT

From the time that the Covenant of Salt God made with King David and his sons was ordained eternal it has occurred continually. And although manifested in different ways, this Covenant of Salt will prove to be of the same substance as:

- The Rainbow Covenant God made with Noah
- The Covenant of Circumcision God made with Abraham
- The Covenant of Peace God speaks of in Isaiah
- The Covenant in Christ's Blood that God has made anew and is now bringing into fulfillment.

Let us now take a look at these specific covenants and how they supernaturally symbolize and reflect God's sanctifying substance salt.

God's Rainbow Covenant: The first sign of God's perpetual and eternal Salt Covenant took place after the flood when God said to Noah: *"This is the sign of the covenant which I give between me and you, and to every living soul that is with you, for perpetual generations I will set my bow in the clouds and it shall be the Sign of a Covenant between me, and between the earth. And when I shall cover the sky with clouds, my bow shall appear in the clouds. And my bow shall be in the clouds and I shall remember the everlasting covenant."* (Genesis 9:12-14)

In pondering these three verses, note how God emphasizes three things, three times:

1. He emphasizes His Covenant three times. Perhaps because the Rainbow Covenant owes its visibility to the three-dimensional crystal salt; three being the number of the Divine Rising.
2. He emphasizes His bow three times. Perhaps because the rainbow, in the shape of a dome, is a sign of the everlasting dominion the Holy Trinity—the Three Persons in One God—desires to have over His people.
3. He emphasizes the clouds three times. The clouds from which proceed the seven colors of the rainbow. The seven colors are a magnificent sign of God's Covenant of Glory that He symbolically sealed with salt and water.

The Seven Colors of the Rainbow: Without the crystal salt the beautiful rainbow of seven colors could not exist. These seven colors are a visual prefiguring of the seven sacraments through which Catholic Priests enable God's people to participate in the fullness of God's life and be crowned with His Eternal Glory.

The number "seven" is woven throughout the Old and New Testaments, it signifies perfection and completion.[72]

It is quite remarkable that in the year 1666 Sir Isaac Newton discovered that when these seven colors of the rainbow are reversed through a "triangular" prism they come out "white." Newton's amazing discovery exemplifies how God uses the natural to reveal

---

72 It is significant that the Catholic Bible has "73" books whereas our Protestant brethren, having removed "7" of these books, have only "66." Our brethren have also turned away from the fullness that dwells in the "7" sacraments of the Church (Martin Luther recognized only two of seven). These 7 sacraments, which have been administered through the Church for over 2000 years, are necessary to bring God's Mystical Body into completion and perfection.

His supernatural plan by allowing us to draw the following remarkable spiritual conclusions:

⁕ The seven colors represent the seven sacraments.
⁕ The triangle prism represents the three Divine Persons in one God—the Most Holy Trinity.
⁕ The "white light," a combination of all seven colors of the visible light spectrum, represents Jesus, who in His Glory (salt and water) appears "dazzling white light!"
⁕ Through God's Glory dispensed to us in the seven sacraments we are washed with the salt and water in the Blood of the Lamb and "robed in white." Of those clothed in Heaven with white robes, the Book of Revelation 7:14 states, *"these are they who are come out of great tribulation, and have washed their robes, and have made them white in the blood of the Lamb."*

(You can see why Sir Isaac Newton believed that the Bible could be interpreted literally.)

The seven colors of the visible light spectrum appear white. Whereas the color black, representing darkness, which is opposite of white and light, is devoid of color and light. The black would therefore represent the horrifying black[73] hole, or dreadful empty void, in which a soul who chooses to refuse the sacraments will anguish for all eternity.

The Circle of Glory: The following beautiful verse on the rainbow is taken from the Book of Ecclesiasticus/Sirach 43:13&14:

"Look upon the rainbow, and bless Him that made it: it is very beautiful in its brightness. It encompasseth the heaven above with the 'circle of its glory,' the hands of the most high have displayed it."

---

73 The seven colors of the visible light spectrum make white light—not to be confused with paint whose seven primary colors make black.

Our beloved God sealed His Rainbow Covenant in His own substance of water and salt which He so beautifully displays in the rainbow circle. The rainbow's ring-shaped circle is a mystical representation of God's engagement ring to His Church. The wedding is taking place through the seven colors which symbolize the seven sacraments that dispense the very substance of God's Glory, represented mystically by His Sanctifying Water and Salt!

We've seen that a secondary rainbow occasionally appears in the sky in which the colors are reversed. The colors in the secondary rainbow, although beautiful, are less vivid. The double rainbow brings to mind a text from Ecclesiaticus 43:24: *"A present remedy for all is the speedy coming of a cloud and the dew that meeteth it."* (Ecclesiasticus 43:24) The first, more brilliant, rainbow represents God's Glory come down from Heaven, whereas the second less vivid rainbow would represent our reception of His Glory in the seven sacraments through which we, like the morning dew, rise up to meet Him.

In the above we have seen how the water and salt displayed in the seven colors[74] of the rainbow promise is a pre-figuration of the water and salt in Christ's Blood dispensed to us in the seven sacraments.

In this same way, the brilliance of these seven sacraments is a pre-figuration of the day soon to come when *"The light of the moon shall be as the light of the sun, and the light of the sun shall be 'seven fold,' as the light of 'seven days': in the day when the Lord shall 'bind' up the wound of His people, and shall heal the stroke of their wound."* (Isaiah 30:26)

Salt is the balm that will cure and restore God's Light to His people. The curing process is brought to perfection through the redemptive process of the seven sacraments which dispense the precious Body and Blood of Christ. This knowledge of the Son of God's

---

74 The gay pride movement has taken the rainbow as their symbol. Their rainbow is always depicted as having six colors!

sanctifying substance will heal, unite, and restore His people, bringing about the *seven fold Light* of the New Jerusalem.

God's Covenant of Circumcision: The second sign of God's perpetual and eternal Salt Covenant was established when God said to Abraham: *"This is my covenant which you shall observe, between me and you, and thy seed after thee: All the male kind of you shall be circumcised: And you shall circumcise the flesh of your foreskin that it may be a sign of the covenant between you and me."* (Genesis 17:10-11)

First consider how circumcision (circular-cut) creates a "dome" in the flesh of the male foreskin. Next think about how the rising of these hidden domes springs forth the substance that gives birth to new life—the salt of the earth. The salt of the earth being God's chosen people of His Salt Covenant—the promise God made with David and his sons to give them the Kingdom over Israel for ever!

(It's also relevant that condoms, which are con-traception, block God's children from coming into existence. The prefix "con" means against, and this is because con-domes are against God's Dominion and Glory.)

These circumcised domes are a sign of the dominion that God desired to have over the seed of Abraham, however in their unbelief the Israelites turned away from God. Therefore, the Lord made a New Salt Covenant that St. Paul tells us is built on *"a better and a lasting substance"* of *"the promise"*—as seen in Hebrews 10:34-35. The better and lasting substance of the promise being the sanctifying substance Salt found in the redemptive Blood of Jesus Christ, the Lamb of God.

These hidden circumcised domes of the flesh also symbolize one of the three rising measures of meal the woman—the Virgin of the Revelation—is preparing. We will come back to this shortly.

God's Covenant of Peace: In Isaiah 55:10 the Lord proclaims: *"For the mountains shall be moved, and the hills shall tremble; but my mercy shall not depart from thee, and the 'covenant of my peace' shall not be moved."*

Another example of the magnitude of salt's spiritual significance is that historically salt symbolized peace. During the Old Salt Covenant people who shared or ate ordinary table salt together during their meals were said to be at peace with one another. This likely came about as a result of the Salt Covenant God made with David and his sons, the Covenant through which God promised them the Kingdom over Israel forever.

This peace that proceeded from sharing salt was a foreshadowing of the everlasting Peace the people who partake of the sanctifying substance salt in the Body and Blood of Christ will come to have. God, whose treasure of mercy is endless, has gifted His people with His everlasting Covenant of Peace.

St. Paul is referring to God's Covenant of Peace when he writes about *"the peace of God which surpasses all understanding"* (Phil. 4:7); the peace by which *"He reconciled all things to Himself making peace through the Blood of the Cross."* (Colossians 1:20)

Jesus breathed on His apostles saying: *Peace I leave with you, my Peace I give unto you* (John 14:27). Jesus' breath, like the wind, blows salt! His breath welling up from the most inner part of His being, the bosom of His Sacred Heart, is on fire with love for each and every one of us. We are now able to enter into a deeper understanding of Jesus' words: *"For everyone shall be salted with fire."* (Mark 9:49)

It's no coincidence the word **Sal**-em means "Place of Peace." Recall the High priest Melchizedek, who foreshadowed Jesus, was King of Salem. In this same way Jesus who is the Prince of Peace is Prince of Salt—the salt of the earth!

Salem foreshadowed Jeru-salem. As is Jeru-salem a foreshadowing of the New Jeru-salem, which is the City of God's Glory—His Salt, His Water and His Light!

It is also no coincidence that the New Jerusalem is also known as the City of David —David being the son of God with whom God made the Covenant of Salt.

The Star of David was the geometric design most used to mine sea salt. In the natural the design of two interconnected triangles allowed the salt in the sea to crystallize over a larger area. In the supernatural this formation represents the interconnectedness of Jesus Christ/Christ Jesus, and the salt from His Precious Blood, crystallizing over all things in heaven and earth. (It is interesting that the figure of a cross in the center of the star was sometimes used to hasten the crystallization of salt.)

The interconnectedness of the triangles is a powerful reminder to us of Jesus' words recorded in John 17:21-23: *"That they all may be one, as thou, Father, in me, and I in thee; that they also may be one in us; that the world may believe that thou has sent me. 'And the glory which thou has given me', I have given to them; that they may be one, as we also are one: I in them, and thou in me; that they may be made perfect in one."* How beautiful!

To recapitulate: Peace = Salt = Salom/Shalom = Salem = Jeru-Salem = The New Jeru-Salem = The City of Peace = The City of David = The City of God's Glory = The City of Salt, Water, and Light.

Of the New Jerusalem St. John in the Book of Revelation 21:10-11, writes: *"And he took me up in Spirit to a great and high mountain: and he showed me the Holy City Jerusalem coming down out of Heaven from God. 'Having the Glory of God' and the 'Light' thereof was like to a precious stone, and as to the jasper stone, even as crystal."*

The Glory of God, as we have seen, mystically consists of the water and salt from His Heavenly Sea from whence came the Cloud of His Glory—the very Cloud of His Glory that overshadowed and impregnated the Virgin Mary with Baby Jesus—the Son of God.

The Salt Covenant Made Anew in Jesus' Blood: God the Father's eternal and perpetual Salt Covenant was made anew with the seed of His Son Jesus' martyrdom. It springs forth from the cut (analogous to an incision) into Jesus' Sacred Heart by the soldier's lance. It is established in Jesus' Blood, perpetually gushing forth from His Sacred Heart.

This covenant is perpetuated through the power of God's anointed Priest sons at the Holy Sacrifice of the Mass where they show the Lord's death until He comes in Glory. (Keep in mind, there is no time or space with God—we are truly present at the foot of the Cross at every Holy Sacrifice of the Mass.) The chalice we drink is filled with the salt of His most precious Blood—it is our cup of salvation!

Audrey Santo (12/19/83 to 4/14/07) is known as the silent victim soul from Worcester, Massachusetts. In her chapel countless miracles have manifested and continue to do so. In the video on Audrey's life "The Story of Little Audrey Santo" we are shown **a chalice that has miraculously filled with Salt!** With permission from Audrey's Bishop, priests come from all over the world to celebrate Holy Mass at this site. The cause for Audrey's beatification is open.

In Matthew 26:27-28 it is written: *"And taking the chalice, He gave thanks, and gave to them, saying drink ye all of this, for this is my Blood of the New Testament [the New Salt Covenant Promise], which shall be shed for many unto remission of sins."*

Dear sisters and brothers in Christ Jesus, the Salt Covenant made anew in the Precious Blood of Jesus is bringing all things into fulfillment through the circumcision of our hearts made contrite and humble through our worthy reception of the seven sacraments.

In retrospect, the salt of the Old Covenant was a foreshadowing of the necessity of the salt in the precious Blood of Jesus to bring about the restoration of God's Kingdom on earth. Recollecting the verse *"Do you not know that the Lord God of Israel gave to David the Kingdom over Israel forever, to him and to his sons by a Covenant of Salt?"* (II Paralipomenon/II Chronicles 13:5)

This scripture speaks volumes, because if God gave David and his sons the Kingdom over Israel forever by a Covenant of Salt, this strongly indicates that salt would be the key that opens the door to the Kingdom—the very Key of David.

The Key of David: The following scripture verses are being repeated due to their profound significance. In them God speaks to Isaiah and also St. John the beloved about the Key of David:

"And I will lay the 'key of the house of David' upon his shoulder: and he shall open and none shall shut: and he shall shut, and none shall open." (Isaiah 22:22)

"And to the angel of the church of Philadelphia, write: These things saith the Holy One and the true one, he that hath the 'key of David,' he that openeth and no man shutteth; shutteth and no man openeth." (Revelation 3:7)

Take note of how the above two verses correspond with the following words Jesus spoke to Peter when giving him the keys to the Kingdom of Heaven:

"And I will give to thee the keys of the kingdom of heaven. And whatsoever thou shalt bind upon earth, it shall be bound also in heaven; and whatsoever thou shalt loose on earth, it shall be loosed also in heaven." (Matthew 16:19)

These verses point to salt as being the mystical key that opens the door to the knowledge of the mystery of God's Kingdom and its rise into wholeness. The very key that is now opening the door of speech to preach the mystery of Christ and His rising within us into fullness.

The Holy Things of David Faithful: Since salt is not only used to preserve things but also to free them from corruption, we are now going to see yet another validating example of how the knowledge of the Covenant of Salt God made with David and his sons is necessary to set us free from corruption.

St. Luke in the Book of the Acts 13:32-34 appears to be writing about the salt covenant promise God made with our Church Fathers and how it is to be fulfilled in Jesus' resurrection. He then writes: *"And to show that He 'raised' Him [Jesus] up from the dead, not to return now any more to 'corruption.' He said thus: I will give you the 'holy things' of faithful David."* Note here how St. Luke links Jesus with the holy things of faithful David, one of which would necessarily be the salt of the covenant through which God promised David and his sons the eternal Kingdom over Israel forever. Keeping in mind that salt is a leaven that raises and also frees things from corruption!

The importance of God's eternal and binding Salt Covenant is further demonstrated in the following verses.

1) *"All the first fruits of the sanctuary, which the children of Israel offer to the Lord, I have given to thee and to thy sons and daughters, by a perpetual ordinance. It is a Covenant of Salt forever before the Lord, to thee and to thy sons."* (Numbers 18:19)
2) *"In all their oblations they shall offer salt. And thou shall offer them in the sight of the Lord: and the priests shall put salt upon them, and shall offer them a holocaust to the Lord."* (Ezekiel 43:24)
3) *"Whatsoever sacrifice thou offerest, thou shalt season it with salt, neither shalt thou take away the salt of the covenant of thy God from thy sacrifice."* (Leviticus 2:13)

Observe how God has ordained that salt be offered perpetually and forever in all His people's sacrifices. This knowledge is of major significance, because, to reiterate, it is through this very Covenant of Salt that God promised David and his sons the Kingdom over Israel "forever".

And yet the Old Salt Covenant apparently ceased with the destruction of the Temple. So does this mean God broke His promise? Absolutely not! The Old Salt Covenant was a foreshadowing of the New Salt Covenant God has made anew in the precious Blood of Jesus.

The oblation of Jesus' Blood is repeated "perpetually" in a mystical way at every Holy Sacrifice of the Mass. In fact, every minute of every day thousands of Masses are being offered by Catholic priests who make present Jesus' sacrifice on the cross. Through this sacrifice Christ's redemptive Body and Blood, gives all glory, honor and praise to God the Father in the Unity of the Holy Ghost. This sacrificial offering contains the better and lasting substance of the promise – the sanctifying salt in the Precious Body and Blood of Jesus! Through this sanctifying salt the Covenant God made with David and his sons is being brought into fulfillment.

(By the way, the prefix "sal" means salt. Thus the words salary and salt are both rooted in salt. This is interesting because the Church teaches that Jesus paid the price for our "salvation", also rooted in salt, with His Precious Blood! The Salt in His Precious Blood!)

The above helps to explain the reason salt was used in the waters of Baptism as well as in Holy Water.

BAPTISM IN SALT AND WATER

Before the Great Consummation of Christ's marriage to His Bride, the Church, can take place His Bride must first be set free from the corruption of sin, because, of course, nothing impure can unite with Christ. This is why salt must be restored to its proper place in the Sacramental Rite.

According to an older edition of <u>The Catholic Encyclopedia</u>[75] the Roman Ritual knows two kinds of salt for liturgical purposes—baptismal salt and blessed salt. It also states that the baptismal salt is cleansed and sanctified by special exorcisms and prayers, and given to the catechumens before they enter church for Baptism. You can also read about the sacred and traditional use of salt at Baptism in <u>The Catechism of the Council of Trent</u> where you will find that a few grains of salt are to be placed in the mouth of the person to be baptized.

---

75 Copyright 1913 by the Encyclopedia Press, Inc.

Now let us look at the compelling significance of salt in the history of our forefathers' Baptism in the cloud and in the sea. Carefully listen to what St. Paul is instructing us on in the following text: *"For I would not have you ignorant brethren, that our fathers were all under the 'cloud', and all passed through the 'sea'. And all in Moses were* **baptized in the cloud; and in the sea.***"* (1 Corinthians 10:1-2) Could Saint Paul have made the importance of salt and water in Baptism any clearer?

You see, it's a fact that salt burns and water can contain an enormous amount of heat. Thus, it makes sense that the special baptismal salt which is "cleansed" and "sanctified" by the following exorcism prayer, when prayed by a priest, acts as a spiritual catalyst to burn and thereby exorcise the corruption of original sin from the soul. Exorcised salt also helps to preserve the soul from future corruption.

These are the words some priests still pray over salt; where you see the cross symbol is when the priest makes the sign of the cross over the salt being blessed.

"O salt, creature of God, I exorcise you by the living (+) God, by the true (+) God, by the holy (+) God, by the God who ordered you to be poured into the water by Elisha the prophet, so that its life-giving powers might be restored. I exorcise you so that you may become a means of salvation for believers, that you may bring health of soul and body to all who make use of you, and that you may put to flight and drive away from the places where you are sprinkled; every apparition, villainy, turn of devilish deceit, and every unclean spirit; adjured by him who will come to judge the living and the dead and the world by fire. Amen.

Let us pray. Almighty and everlasting God, we humbly implore you, in your immeasurable kindness and love, to bless (+) this salt which you created and gave to the use of mankind, so that it may become a source of health for the minds and bodies of all who make use of it. May it rid whatever it touches or sprinkles of all uncleanness, and protect it from every assault of evil sprits. Through Christ our Lord. Amen."

It is significant that John the Baptist baptized Jesus in the Jordan River which has a high mineral content of salt. In fact, the Jordan River[76] could not be used for farming without the use of dams and drainage canals specifically installed to dissolve the salt from the soil and water. It is also relevant that the Jordan River runs through the Sea of Galilee, which is actually a lake but called a sea because of its high salt content. The Jordan River is the site of many events and miracles in the life of Jesus.

It is also noteworthy that both St. John the Baptist and St. Patrick are often traditionally depicted baptizing with a seashell in hand and that many baptismal fonts were made in the shape of a seashell[77].

---

76 Blessed Anne Catherine Emmerich in <u>The Life of Jesus Christ and Biblical Revelations</u>, Vol. 1 pg. 140, writes about seeing a cloud coming down from Heaven and dispersing into the Jordan River.

77 As is the one presently used at the Basilica of St. Lawrence during the Easter Season; and also the one used during Ordinary Time which has on its cover a figure of St. John the Baptist baptizing Jesus with a seashell in hand! The Basilica also has a huge statue of St. Patrick, who is holding a three-leaf clover in one hand and a "seashell" in the other - the seashell is meant to symbolize the many thousands St. Patrick baptized!

This traditional imagery of a SEAshell suggests the propriety of using salt in the waters of Baptism, does it not?

And is it not fascinating that St. Augustine would say that he tasted the salt of God in his mother's womb?[78]

Isn't it also intriguing that in Leonardo daVinci's depiction of the Last Supper, Judas Iscariot is portrayed as having ominously spilt the salt shaker!?!

Salt, the Two-Edged Sword: The Jordan River empties into the Dead Sea which is composed of approximately 27% salt. Nothing can live in the Dead Sea with the exception of plants that grow only in salty soil called <u>hal</u>ophytes. The prefix "hal" like the prefix sal, is defined as "more at salt" and will prove very meaningful.

The Dead Sea, the lowest body of water on earth, is the site where God rained fire and brimstone down on Sodom and Gomorrah. This is a reminder that God's Word is living and effectual, sharper than a two-edged sword, indicating that salt will either bring you to eternal life or to eternal damnation![79]

The Dead Sea salt is a paradox for those who in this "last time" refuse to serve God. Those who put the creature before the Creator as well as those who live lifestyles of sexual perversion – read Romans Chapter One to see for your self these prevalent signs of our times. Pay particular attention to Verse 32, which forewarns: *"…that they who do such things, are worthy of death; and not only they that do them, but also that consent to them that do them."*

Of the Dead Sea salt it is written: *"Burning it with brimstone and the heat of salt, so that it cannot be sown [the evil seed] anymore."* (Deuteronomy 29:23)

---

78 St. Francis de Sales, <u>Introduction to the Devout Life,</u> pg. 260.

79 Calling to mind the "good" medicinal use of Normal Saline to save life, verses the "evil" lethal use of saline solutions to abort life.

St. John the Baptist declared *"I indeed baptize with water...He [Jesus] shall baptize you with the Holy Ghost and Fire."* (Luke 3:16) And yet Scripture tells us that Jesus did not baptize[80]—so how is this possible? Because the Baptism with which Jesus (our priests in Persona Christi) baptizes comes from the Blood of His Cross!

In the Roman Rite, Baptism into the Mystical Body of Christ traditionally made use of sanctified and exorcised water as well as sanctified and exorcized salt. This is not meant to imply that Baptism without the use of the exorcised and sanctified salt would not be a valid Baptism—remember that clean water owes its visibility to the substance salt. However, it is meant to imply that the use of the sanctified and exorcised substance salt in the waters of Baptism is more efficacious, and that the revelation of this knowledge of the mystical connection between the Son of God and sanctified Salt is necessary to bring God's Mystical Body into unity and perfection, ushering in the New Spring Time Saint John Paul II prophesied. In the same way Eliseus/Elisha poured salt into the spring of the waters of the Jordan thereby freeing the waters of the spring from death and barrenness.

Perhaps you are old enough to recall when the exorcised and sanctified substance salt was a mandatory part of the Sacramental Rite of Baptism for Catholics of the Roman Rite. This was back when Catholics were a faithful people; back when they believed, loved, and adored the True Presence of Jesus in the Eucharist[81]; back when there were lines at the confessional; back when the majority of the holy and solemn vows of Matrimony and Holy Orders were honored for a lifetime. Those were the days when the Church's Magisterium

---

80 John 4:2: *Though Jesus himself did not baptize, but his disciples*

81 Polls show only 30% of Catholics believe in the True Presence of Jesus in the Eucharist – how shockingly sad is this!

and God's Commandments were respected and reverenced by most Catholics.

The Prophet Ezekiel from the Old Covenant also testifies to the necessary use of salt in the water of Baptism. In the following verse God is speaking metaphorically of the Old Jerusalem while instructing Ezekiel to inform her, the Old Jerusalem, of the reasons for her abominations: *"And when thou wast born, in the day of thy nativity thy navel was not cut, 'neither was thou washed with water for thy health, nor salted with salt, nor swaddled with clouts. No eye had pity on thee to do any of these things for thee out of compassion for thee: but thou wast cast out upon the face of the earth in the abjection of thy soul, in the day that thou was born."* (Ezekiel 16:4&5) God spoke these words to declare the necessity of water, salt, and humility (clout/rag) to bring about Jerusalem's rebirth into the New Jerusalem!

Yet our Church liturgists no longer require the blessed and exorcised salt to be used in the Sacrament of Baptism—nor even the use of blessed salt in Holy Water. Could this indicate that the *Key of Knowledge*[82] that the lawyers took away and Jesus came to restore has once again been taken from the people? Could this point to one of the reasons the Church is suffering so much?

Let us hear what God has to say about the rejection of His knowledge: *"Because thou hast rejected knowledge [the key of knowledge] I will reject thee that thou shall not do the office of priesthood to me and thou hast forgotten the law [salt law, as seen in Leviticus 2:13] of thy God, I also will forget thy children. According to the multitude of them so have they sinned against me: I will change their glory into shame."* (Osee/Hosea 4:6-7)

Could the rejection of the blessed and exorcised substance salt from the waters of the Sacrament of Baptism, as well as from the

---

82 Luke 11:52

Church's sacramental's, pinpoint when corruption entered the Church?

It is important to understand that the mysteries of the fullness of Faith have been preserved by the Roman Catholic Church where the Keys to the Kingdom of God's Sea of Heavenly Glory were entrusted to St. Peter. These Keys have been preserved down through the ages by the Church's Magisterium – teaching authority. This is the reason why good and holy priests and nuns of days gone by drilled into the heads of their students: "Never forget you are a Roman Catholic[83]!" These holy religious were given the knowledge and wisdom to understand that the Catholic Church is the One Holy Catholic and Apostolic Church through which God will bring all things into perfection and completion. It does so through its teachings built on the solid rock foundation of both Holy Tradition[84] and Sacred Scripture: Holy Tradition which has preserved the efficacious use of the exorcised and sanctified substance salt in the Sacrament of Baptism; and Sacred Scripture which necessitates the use of water in the Sacrament of Baptism.

As Catholics, we have the blessed assurance that God reveals Himself to us both through Sacred Scripture and through Holy Tradition.

THE SPIRITUAL DRINK AND THE SPIRITUAL ROCK

Jesus Christ – the Rock Salt of our Salvation: After emphasizing our forefathers' Baptism in water and salt, the cloud and the sea, St. Paul writes *"And all drank the same spiritual drink, and they*

---

83 This is meant to include and acknowledge all twenty-two rites of the Church which are united in their common bond to the successor of St. Peter, the Pope of Rome.
84 See II Thes. 2:14: *Therefore, brethren, stand fast; and hold the traditions which you have learned, whether by word, or by our epistle.*

drank of the spiritual rock that followed them, and the rock was Christ." (I Corinthians 10:4) The spiritual "drink" signifies God the Father – the Fountain of Living Water; the spiritual "rock" signifies God the Son, whose sanctifying substance salt is, as we shall see, mystically represented by rock salt.

The spiritual drink and the spiritual rock are the water and salt our spirits and souls are washed, preserved, and sanctified through, with, and in the seven sacraments.

Jesus Changes Simon's Name to Peter Meaning Rock. When Jesus called Simon, a fisherman, to become a fisher of men he changed His name to Peter, which means, "rock." He said to Peter: "*Thou art Peter, and **upon this rock** I will build my Church, and the gates of hell shall not prevail against it. And I will give to thee the 'keys' of the Kingdom of heaven. And whatsoever thou shalt bind upon earth, it shall be bound also in heaven; and whatsoever thou shalt loose on earth, it shall be loosed also in heaven.*" (Matthew 16:18-19) Jesus changed Simon's name to Peter, meaning rock, because a rock in the Old Salt Covenant was a visible sign of God's strength, but even more importantly because He was giving Peter the key to the knowledge of His "hidden" rock salt the key-stone upon which He would build His Church.

The Three Hidden and Rising Rock Salt Domes

The leavening ingredient the woman, the Virgin of the Revelation, in the parable of Matthew 13:33, has hidden in the three measures of meal has been shown to be salt. The woman is now revealing the knowledge of the secret rising ingredient because, as indicated by the parable, her meal is about to rise into wholeness. With this in mind, we are going to look at some pretty spectacular information on how these three hidden and rising measures of meal can also be likened to: 1) the world 2) the flesh and, 3) the spirit.

In a most surprising way we are going to see how the rising up of salt from within the world, the flesh, and the spirit, is indicative of what is to bring about the great consummation Jesus is speaking about in Matthew 24:14, *"And this Gospel of the Kingdom, shall be preached in the whole world, for a testimony to all nations, and then shall the consummation come."* The consummation is also mentioned in the Old Covenant Book of Daniel 9:27, *"And he [the antichrist] shall confirm the [false] covenant with many, in one week; and in the half of the week the victim and the sacrifice shall fail; and there shall be in the temple the abomination of desolation; and the desolation shall continue even to the consummation, and to the end."*

We will now see how salt, hidden within the three measures of the world, the flesh, and the spirit—is giving rise to this great consummation; and not only is it giving rise to this consummation, but in all three instances it is rising in the shape of a dome.

The Consummation of the World: It's a scientific fact that rock salt, hidden in many underground places throughout the earth, is rising up in the shape of a dome. In fact, there is a rock salt dome underground in Louisiana[85] that is even larger than Mount Everest the highest mountain peak in the world. Imagine that! It's also a scientific fact that the rising of these hidden rock salt domes is creating geological stresses—known as faults, in the earth's strata. It's quite plausible that these geological stresses construct the catalyst that induces the great earthquake prophesied in the Book of Revelation 8:5 and 11:19.

---

85 The Avery Island rock salt dome is located 140 miles west of New Orleans.

As you read the following three scripture verses think about how the rising and gushing forth of the hidden rock salt domes from within the earth are relevant to them.

* In Deuteronomy 29:23-25 we see where those who *"forsake the Covenant"* (God's Salt Covenant) shall be burned with *"brimstone, and the heat of salt!"* (Making the point that salt is the mystical two-edged sword that will either bring us into eternal life or eternal damnation!)

* In Mark 9:48 Jesus states, *"For every one shall be 'salted' with fire: and every victim shall be 'salted' with 'salt.'"* (Mark 9:49) (When this salting with fire comes, the children of God's Salt Covenant will lovingly embrace the fire of His sanctifying Salt. Whereas Satan and his cohorts, who are diametrically opposed to God, will burn in anguish.)

* Then in 2 Peter 3:7, St. Peter instructs us that this earth (the second earth in which we now live) is *"reserved unto 'fire' against the day of judgment."*

This salting with fire is necessary to purify the second Heaven and earth in which we now live, transforming it anew into the Third Heaven and Earth—the New Jerusalem, in which God's Dominion, His Divine Will, shall reign.

The following picture is a cross section of the Avery Island salt dome.

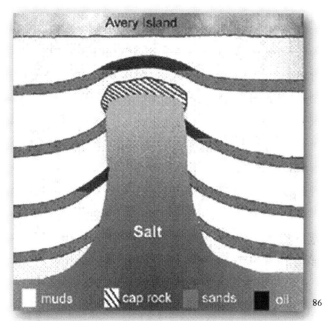

Note the shape of this rising salt dome, could this image represent yet another example of God using the visible to give birth to His invisible plan?

The Consummation of the Flesh: Now we look at how the consummation of the flesh is reflected in the gospel of circumcision which was given to St. Peter to preach: *"But contrariwise, when they had seen that to me [St. Paul] was committed the gospel of uncircumcision, as to 'Peter was that of the circumcision."* (Galatians' 2:7)

Circumcision is the sign of the perpetual and everlasting Covenant God made with Abraham and his seed and established with His following Word:

* *"And I will establish my covenant between me and thee, and between thy seed after thee in their generations, by a 'perpetual covenant:' to be a God to thee, and to thy seed after thee."* (Genesis 17:7)

---

86 From the website www.marin.edu

⁕ Then three verses later: *"This is my covenant which you shall observe, between me and you, and thy seed after thee: All the male kind of you shall be circumcised: And you shall circumcise the flesh of your foreskin that it may be a sign of the covenant between you and me."* (Genesis 17:10-11)

Think about how circumcision cuts into the foreskin of the male anatomy and removes the outermost flesh, the part from which new life springs forth—creating a fresh new foreskin in the shape of a dome. This symbolizes:

⁕ The cut—the consummation of the flesh.
⁕ The new foreskin—the birth of the new man.
⁕ The dome—the dominion God desires to have over man.

Keeping in perspective how God uses the visible to reveal His invisible plan of salvation, ponder how in the same way the hidden and rising salt domes of the world are to spring forth and give birth to the New Heavens and Earth, so too do the hidden and rising circumcised domes of the flesh spring forth salt. The very salt of the earth Jesus is referring to in Matthew 5:13 when He says: *"You are the salt of the earth!"*

(*The revelation of this truly amazing knowledge is supported by the Catechism of the Catholic Church, section 704, wherein it is stated: "God fashioned man with His own hands (that is the Son and the Holy Spirit) and impressed His own form on the flesh He had fashioned, in such a way that even what is visible might bear the Divine form.")

These rising circumcised domes give "new birth" to the children of God's *salt* promise, the better and more lasting substance of the Covenant that He made with David and his sons. The Salt Covenant through which He promised them the Kingdom over Israel forever and is now bringing into fulfillment with the Salt in His beloved Son's most precious Body and Blood.

The Consummation of the Spirit: The consummation of the spirit is brought forth through the knowledge of "the Gospel of Uncircumcision," which has been given to St. Paul to preach *"as to me was committed the gospel of uncircumcision."* (Galatians 2:7)

This gospel of God's Mystical Kingdom also springs forth from a cut made into the flesh—the lance that pierced Jesus' Heart. We enter into covenant with Jesus when we partake of the sanctifying substance salt springing forth from the Blood of His Sacred Heart. His Sacred Heart which pumps perpetually with excesses of profound Love & Mercy for each one of us.

This mystical <u>salt</u> is the rock upon which God is bringing His Church under His dominion – into perfection and completion. This <u>hidden</u> salt, dispensed to us in the seven sacraments, is now <u>rising</u> up from within our double <u>domed</u> shaped hearts.

Through the seven sacraments we partake of God's Glory—the everlasting Water and sanctifying Salt from the Heavenly Sea of His Kingdom of Glory.

The preaching of the Gospel of the Glory of God's Kingdom will bring about the "mystical consummation" of Christ's Marriage to His Church. This consummation also gives new birth—to God's children of "light" (water + salt = Light), our glorified new life in the New Jerusalem!

This is the "gospel of uncircumcision" committed to St. Paul's trust to preach. Recall how when St. Paul asks that a door of speech be opened to him to preach the mystery of Christ he no sooner says *"Let your speech be seasoned with salt so that you know how to answer men."*

The knowledge of salt being revealed helps us to enter into an even deeper understanding of these words Jesus uses to describe the blessed as: *"the salt of the earth and the light of the world!"* (Matthew 5:13). In Mark 9:49 Jesus clearly states, *"Have salt in you, and have peace among you."*

Back to the parable: The woman—the Virgin of the Revelation—is now revealing the knowledge of these three hidden and rising salt domes[87] because salt is the ingredient she hid in the three measures of the bread dough (the world, the flesh, and the spirit) that she has been preparing—the very ingredient whose knowledge thereof, per the parable, will bring about the rising of Her meal into wholeness/fullness.

The Secret Mystery

The Secret Mystery: When St. Paul in Romans 16:25 writes about *"the revelation of **the mystery kept secret** for all eternity,"* he is referring to the hidden knowledge of the Mystery of Christ's Second Coming—the Gospel of Christ's Glory—that is now being manifested to the saints. It is essential to keep this in mind because it is the "unveiling" of the knowledge (the key of knowledge) of this mystery kept secret for all eternity that the woman—The Virgin of the Revelation—is *"now,"* in what St. Paul calls *"due time,"* revealing/unveiling.

Call to mind how Our Lady appeared under the title "The Virgin of the Revelation" in the square of Three Fountains, Rome, at the site where St. Paul was decapitated. Recollect that during this

---

87 As the author was given the word of knowledge on these three hidden and rising rock salt domes, imagine her astonishment when she learned that not far from her home witches had succeeded in evading the covenants in a restricted neighborhood and were in the process of building a "three domed" residence!

apparition she gave the seer, Bruno Cornocchiola, a "secret message" for the Pope, who at the time was Pius XII.

Secret Message—Secret Words—Kept Secret—Made Secret: It's logical that the Virgin of the Revelation's "secret message" for the Pope would have something to do with the title under which she appeared — "Revelation." And since her apparition took place on the grounds where St. Paul was decapitated, it's also consistent that the secret message would correspond to *"the Revelations of Christ"* that St. Paul was given when he was taken up into the Third Heaven and heard *"secret words,"* as seen in 2 Corinthians 12:1-4.

This appears to also indicate that the "secret message" given for the Pope would have something to do with what St. Paul writes about as, *"...the preaching of Jesus Christ according to 'the revelation of the mystery of Christ' which was 'kept secret' from eternity."* (Romans 16:25)

Moreover, this secret message would also likely correspond to what Jesus is referring to in the following as "made secret," *"For there is nothing hid [in the bread dough by the woman of Matthew 13:33] which shall not be made manifest, neither was it 'made secret,' but that it may come abroad."* (Mark 4:22) Indeed it has come abroad to the United States of America.

(Under the title "Our Lady of the America's," the Blessed Mother desires to once again bless our country through an image of herself under this title, displayed and venerated in the Basilica of the Immaculate Conception in Washington, DC.)

Saint John Paul II: The two saints who were given the revelations of Jesus Christ—the Apostles John and Paul—were both, per Sacred Scripture, given these unveilings of Jesus while taken into the future. It is therefore providential that Saint John Paul the Great embraced the names of these two great saints whose revelations of Jesus Christ are now being manifested.

With this in mind it's plausible that the secret message the Virgin of the Revelation gave Bruno to give to the Pope was that the revelation of the Mystery of Jesus Christ and His rise into fullness would soon be manifested. This would also explain why Pope John Paul II as we approached the millennium, informed us that we could anticipate a revelation of Jesus Christ to be made known. He also said that we could expect something new to be made clear about God.

As pertains to the works of our merciful Father in Heaven, Saint John Paul II also prophesied: "He is now doing something new, and in the love which forgives[88] He anticipates the New Heavens and the New Earth!" Then to our Father in Heaven the Pope prayed: "Father, by the power of the Spirit, strengthen the Church's commitment to the 'new evangelization' and guide our steps along the pathways of the world, to proclaim Christ by our lives, and to direct our earthly pilgrimage towards the City of Heavenly Light."[89]

The New Evangelization Saint John Paul II has called into being (*"Calleth those things that are not, as those they are."* Romans 4:17) is the preaching of St. Paul's Gospel of the Glory of Christ.

The Gospel of Christ's Glory which has been committed to St. Paul's trust and is now being unveiled by the Virgin of the Revelation is what will give **rise** to the Third Heaven and Earth. In this New Heaven and Earth the King's Dominion – God's Holy and Divine Will – reigns. The preaching of this New Evangelization—to every

---

88 In the Gospel of Matthew, Peter poses the question to Jesus: *Lord, how often shall my brother offend against me, and I forgive him? Till seven times?* (18:21) Jesus responds: *I say not to thee, till seven times; but till seventy times seven times* (18:22). The number "7" also corresponds to forgiveness, because forGIVING is a necessary requirement for us to RECEIVE entry into the New Heavens and the New Earth.

89 This is an excerpt from Saint Pope John Paul II's prayer for the Great Jubilee Year.

nation, and people, and tongue and king—answers Vatican II's call for Universal Holiness.

This, dear saints, is the threshold we must cross to enter into *"The LIGHT of the GOSPEL of the GLORY of CHRIST."* (2 Cor. 4:4) The preaching of the Gospel of the Glory of Christ, as unveiled herein, directs our pilgrimage to its happy ending—the New Jerusalem—the City of God's Peace, Love, Joy and Light.

CHAPTER 6

§

"Beware Ye of the Leaven of the Pharisees
For there is nothing covered that shall not be revealed:
Nor hidden,
that shall not be made known."

LUKE 12:1-2

Yeast - The Leaven of the Pharisees
(Luke 12:1)

THE LEAVEN OF THE PHARISEES that is giving rise to the kingdom of darkness is "yeast"—a fungus that lacks chlorophyll from the sun's light. Whereas, the leaven giving rise to God's Kingdom of Light is "salt" from the Son's Light!

When the Gospel of the Glory of Christ's Kingdom is proclaimed and preached, the yeast of the Pharisees—will rise up against the Salt of the earth.

Jesus' was speaking of this day in time when He said: *"For nation shall rise against nation, and kingdom [of darkness] against kingdom [of light]; and there shall be pestilences, and famines, and earthquakes in places."* (Matthew 24:7). *"And this 'Gospel of the Kingdom' shall be preached in the whole world, for a 'testimony' to all nations, and then shall the consummation come."* (Matthew 24:14)

The fact that yeast is a fungus that lacks chlorophyll from the sun's light explains why the Hebrew people, in readying themselves to partake of the unblemished sacrificial lamb on the Feast of Passover, could not use any yeast in their cooking. (By the way, the Feast of Passover commenced the seven days Feast of Unleavened Bread.) Indeed, they had to search their homes meticulously for any sign of yeast, a sign of sin and darkness, and then dispose of it before Passover began.

In this same way, the Church requires that we search ourselves— temples of the Living God, for any sign of sin or darkness before we enter into the New Passover— the Holy Sacrifice of the Mass. This is because at the Holy Sacrifice of the Mass we partake of Jesus the unblemished Lamb of God—veiled in the unleavened bread.

CHAPTER 7

"In whom the god of this world hath blinded the minds of unbelievers,
that the light of
THE GOSPEL OF THE GLORY OF CHRIST,
who is the image of God,
should not shine unto them."

2 Corinthians 4:4

The Gospel of the Glory of Christ
2 Corinthians 4:4

DEAR SAINTS IN CHRIST JESUS, the word Glory appears approximately 468 times in the Bible. In the New Covenant it is written approximately 150 times, and about as many as one third of these times it is used in the phrase *"the glory of God,"* as seen in: John 11:40; Romans 5:2 & 15:7; 2 Corinthians 1:20, 4:6 & 4:15; and Revelation 15:8. Next we also see it used in the context of *"the glory of God the Father,"* as seen in: Mark 8:38; Luke 9:29; and Philippians 2:11. Then again in the context of *"the crown of glory,"* as seen in: Hebrews 2:9 and 1 Peter 5:4. As a final example we see it spoken of as: *"the riches of God's glory,"* as seen in: Ephesians 1:16; Philippians 4:1; and Colossians 1:27.

This sample of the word Glory's usage in the Bible is given to illustrate the powerful significance that lies in the knowledge of the "substance" of God's Glory—salt and water—now being made known.

Jesus, the Brightness of God's Glory, the figure of God's substance: As we have seen, God's sanctifying substance salt entered the world via the Cloud of His Glory that overshadowed the Immaculate Virgin Mary, the very Cloud through which the Virgin conceived the Son of God—Jesus. Jesus, who in becoming man, gave "figure"—to God's "substance" of Glory, as seen in Hebrews 1:3: *"Who, being the brightness of God's Glory, 'the figure of His substance."*

As a matter of fact, the knowledge of the substance of God's Glory, which gave figure in Jesus, is so meaningful that St. Paul calls it a Gospel:

"In whom the god of this world hath blinded the minds of unbelievers that the light of 'the Gospel of the Glory of Christ,' who is the 'image of God,' should not shine unto them." (2 Corinthians 4:4)

Since the Glory of Christ is a Gospel, then the very knowledge of the figure of God's substance of Glory—the life giving Water and sanctifying Salt in the precious Body and Blood of Jesus—must be made known and preached by the Church to the universal world.

St. Paul continues:

"For God who hath commanded the light to shine out of darkness, hath shined in our hearts, to give 'the light of the knowledge of the glory of God', in the face of Christ Jesus." (2 Cor. 4:6)

Dearly beloved, the face of Christ Jesus is the face of God's beloved priest sons within whom God has invested and sealed Himself. When these courageous Marian Priests preach the knowledge of the Gospel of the Glory of Christ, the light of God's Glory is going to shine ever so brightly in their faces. Those who embrace this knowledge with their hearts when it is preached will see the light of God's Glory manifest in the faces of these true and faithful priest sons of God.

The preaching of *"the Gospel of the Glory of Christ"* to the whole world must take place in order to bring about the consummation of Christ's Marriage to His Church. Jesus was speaking of this very Gospel of His King-dome when He said: *"And this Gospel of the Kingdom shall be preached to the whole world, as a testimony to all nations, and then shall the consummation come."* (Matthew 24:14)

Bear in mind that the Gospels of Matthew, and Mark, and Luke and John proclaim the life and Glory of the Son of God—Our Lord and Savior Jesus Christ, whereas St. Paul's gospel, which was hidden and is only now in the last time being unveiled, is about the life and Glory of the sons of God—within whom Christ Jesus is now rising into fullness.

THE SUBSTANCE OF GOD'S GLORY

The Beginning of His Substance: My dear sisters and brothers, in order to be partakers of Christ, St. Paul explicitly states that we must hold the beginning of His substance firm to the end: *"For we are made partakers of Christ: yet so, if we hold 'the beginning of His substance' firm to the end."* (Hebrews 3:14)

To rediscover the critical knowledge of the "beginning of Christ's substance," we need only go to the beginning of God's Word – the first chapter and verses of the Bible:

Genesis 1:2: *"and the Spirit of God moved over the **water**…"* (Note that God does not say that He created the water – but rather He "moved" over the water.)

Genesis 1:3: *"And God said: Be **light** made…"* (Water & salt = light)

Genesis 1:10: *"and the gathering together of the waters He called the **seas**."*

As you can see, it is precisely in the very beginning of God's Word that the knowledge of God's beginning substance—the Light of His life giving water and sanctifying salt which He called the seas—is revealed. Thus, we can say that we are made partakers of Christ if we hold the beginning of His water and salt firm to the end!

The First Elements: In Hebrew 5:12, St. Paul is referring to the beginning of Christ's substance when he writes about "the first elements": *"For whereas for the time you ought to be masters, you have need to be 'taught again' what are 'the first elements' of the Words of God."*

These first elements of the Words of God would naturally correspond to His beginning substance as revealed above in Genesis 1:2-10. Therefore, the first elements we have need of being taught again would be the water and salt from the Sea of His Light. These must be *"taught again"* because it is through the knowledge of the mystical meaning of these first elements of God's Glory, water and salt, that we will not only be set free from the corruption of the world but also from death and barrenness. As foreshadowed when Eliseus/Elisha poured salt from a new vessel into the "spring waters" of the Jordan and healed them of death or barrenness.

The Things that were First: In the Book of Isaiah 42:9, God mentions *the things that were first.* He then goes on to say that He will declare *new things* which He will make us hear before they *spring forth.* Listen with your hearts:

> *"The things that were first', behold they are come: and 'new things' do I declare: Before they 'spring forth' I will make you hear them."*

As we reflect on this meaningful verse we are now able to deduce:

* *"The Things that were first"* would naturally coincide with "the *beginning of His substance"* and *"the first elements."* Therefore, they too are the water and salt, the seas, of God's Light."

- *"The New Things"* are the renewal of the new spirit, the new flesh, and the new world, which will come into existence through our being taught again the light of the knowledge of the purifying water and sanctifying salt, the very elements of the figure of God's substance of Glory.
- God is *"now"* making us *"hear"* these *"new things"* because they are about to *"spring forth"* into what Saint John Paul II prophesied as "the New Spring-time!"

In this New Spring-Time, God's off-spring will have been made crystal clear through the knowledge of salt and water from the Seas of His Light. (Light=Love=Life.)

The salt and water being: the figure of His beginning substance; the first elements; the things that were first; the new things He is now declaring because they are about to spring forth!

In 1Peter 1:12-14, St. Peter is referring to "these things" which God, in the above, said He would "declare" before they spring forth, when he writes *"those things which are 'now' being 'declared' to you."* (Scripture interprets Scripture)

The light of the knowledge of the Gospel of the Glory of Christ is the very knowledge of God that St. Paul prays we increase in: *"That you may walk worthy of God, in all things pleasing, being fruitful in every good work and 'increasing in the knowledge of God."* (Colossians 1:10) It is this very knowledge of God's Glory that he is instructing us to be renewed in, *"And putting on the new man, him who is 'renewed in knowledge,' according to the' image of Him' that created him."* (Colossians 3:10)

<u>The New Things about to "Spring Forth" were foreshadowed by the Three Springs which sprang forth where St. Paul's head bounced when decapitated:</u> This wonderful knowledge fits the mosaic being

pieced together beautifully because the three springs which sprang forth where St. Paul's head was decapitated and bounced three times, like all water, originate from God the Fountain of Living Water, who, being everywhere, permeates all things.

These three springs would therefore represent the indwelling waters of the spirit, the flesh, and the world,[90] whose waters, as we know, have become polluted and are in need of a healing remedy. This is precisely why St. Paul calls himself a doctor,[91] he knows he has the prescription, the salt remedy, which is necessary to cure and restore these springs to crystal clearness.

Another scripture from the Old Covenant that demonstrates the power in salt's ability to "heal" is found in Ezekiel 47:1-8. Here we read about the rising of the waters issuing forth from the Temple: *"These 'waters' that issue forth toward the hillocks of sand to the east, and go down to the plains of the desert, shall 'go into the sea,' and shall go out, 'and the waters shall be healed."*

The Temple symbolizes God and the waters symbolize His off-spring. Note how these waters must go into the sea to be healed—salt being the healing remedy. The lesson to be taught and learned, once again, is that it is the knowledge of the salt from God's heavenly Sea of Glory, dispensed to us through the seven sacraments of the Church, that will set us free the defilement of the world and bring about our restoration into wholeness.

---

90 From the depths within, St. Augustine in his book Confessions, spoke these words to our immutable God, "And, lo! My infancy died long since, and I live. But Thou, Lord, Who for ever livest, and in Whom nothing dies; for before the foundation of the worlds, and before all that can be called 'before,' Thou art, and art God and Lord of all which Thou hast created; in Thee abide, fixed for ever, the first causes of all things unabiding; and of all things changeable, the springs abide in Thee unchangeable, and in Thee live the eternal reason s of all things unreasoning and temporal."

91 I Timothy 2:7

TAUGHT AGAIN; PROPHESY AGAIN; GLORIFY AGAIN; RISEN AGAIN!

Another important comparison that should be made about the first elements of the Words of God that St. Paul instructs us must *"taught again,"* is to connect what we must be taught again with the prophecy that St. John tells us must be *"prophesied again' to many nations, and peoples, and tongues, and kings."* (Revelations 10:11)

This connection is critical to make because these elements that must be taught again and this prophecy that must be prophesied again—is what is necessary to <u>bring about the glorification of God the Father's name *"again."*</u> (John 12:28)

Here it is good to take to heart these intense words Jesus spoke to God the Father when the hour for His passion and death had come, *"Now is my soul troubled. And what shall I say? Father, save me from this hour. But for this cause I came unto this hour. 'Father, glorify thy name.' A voice therefore came from heaven: I have both glorified it, and will 'glorify it again."* (John 12:27-28)

Dearly beloved, Jesus Christ's primary[92] mission was, and is, to glorify His Father's Name, which He has done, and will do again. The second glorification of the Father's Name will come about through the suffering, death, and resurrection of Christ Jesus, invested and sealed in God the Father's beloved Marian Priest Sons.

This second glorification of the Father's Name takes place through the Marian Priests when they proclaim throughout the universal world "the Gospel of the Glory of Christ" – now being unveiled. This knowledge enters these holy and devout chosen and beloved Priest Sons of God into their hour of darkness. It is primarily for this cause that they, like Jesus, have entered into the world.

---

92 Jesus' primary mission was, and is, to declare His Father's name as foreseen when God the Father declared to Pharaoh, *For this purpose have I raised thee, that I may show my power in thee,* **and that '*my name*' may be '*declared*' throughout the world** (Romans 9:17).

Priest sons of God, prepare and dispose yourselves to *"Bring to the Lord glory and honor, bring to the Lord the glory of His Name: Adore ye the Lord in His holy court."* (Psalm 29:2)

We should know that the word "glorify" is synonymous with "hallow." This is important because the one prayer Jesus taught His disciples/us to pray invokes us to glorify Our Father's Name: *"Our Father Who art in heaven hallowed be thy Name thy Kingdom come."* Notice how these words of prayer reveal to us that when the Father's name is glorified, as it will be again through His beloved Marian Priest Sons, His Kingdom comes!

How fascinating it is that the hallowing of Our Father's Name also proves to be rooted in salt, the prefix "hal" is defined as "salt!" Hal, like the prefix sal, means salt!

And finally, because everything must come full circle:

- The first elements that must be **taught again**
- and this prophesy that must be **prophesied again**
- brings about the hallowing/glorification of **the Father's Name again**
- …which brings about Christ, in us, **risen again!**

St. Paul tells us we are: *"Buried with Him in Baptism, in whom also you are 'risen again' by the faith of the operation of God, who hath raised Him up from the dead."* (Colossians 1:12) Correspondingly, in 2 Timothy 2:8 he writes, *"Be mindful that the Lord Jesus Christ is 'risen again' from the dead, of the seed of David, 'according to my gospel."* (2 Timonthy 2:8) We must keep in mind that St. Paul's Gospel of the Glory of Christ is written from a futuristic perspective (remember he was born out of due time) where he sees the Light (salt and water), as in Glory, of the Lord Jesus Christ—in us—risen again! Glory, Glory, Halleluiah!

And finally, the word "again" calls to mind Ecclesiastes 3:15: *"Things that shall be, have already been, and God restoreth that which is past."* This is because everything that happened to Jesus Christ must happen "again" to Christ Jesus—who lives, moves and has His being within His people, His beloved children.

(A teaching of Father Joachim's: As Paul received all his visions and revelations of the Lord when he was 'caught up into the Third Heaven' all his letters pertain to and should be read in the Light of the Mystery of Jesus' Second Coming, including all the redeeming work of Christ Jesus.)

CHAPTER 8

"Dearly beloved,
think not strange the burning heat which is to try you,
as if some new thing happened to you;
But if you partake of the sufferings of Christ,
rejoice that when His glory shall be revealed,
you may also be glad with exceeding joy."

I PETER 4:12-13

The Basilica Domes of St. Lawrence and St. Peter

§

IT IS PROVIDENTIAL THAT THE knowledge of the Gospel of Christ's Glory is: 1) Emerging from under a dome. 2) The dome forms the roof of a Basilica. 3) The Basilica is named after St. Lawrence. 4) The Basilica Coat of Arms includes an image of the Keys to the Kingdom of Heaven. 5) The architect and builder of the Basilica, is named after St. Raphael. 6) And finally, that this unveiling is associated with St. Francis. The following reasons testify to these facts being of a providential nature.

St. Lawrence Basilica

Completed in 1909 the Basilica of St. Lawrence has the largest, freestanding, elliptical dome in the USA—measuring 82 feet by 58 feet. Until recently it was believed that this dome was impossible to duplicate—and it is yet to be proven otherwise. It was not surprising to learn from a historical preservation engineer that as Raphael Guastavino, architect and builder of the Basilica, progressed in building the dome he added 1% salt to each layer, every 17 inches, of tile and mortar. Is it possible that salt is the substance of cohesion that bound the dome together?

A Basilica is a Roman Catholic Church that is given certain liturgical privileges from its Patriarchal Church of Rome, St. Peter's Basilica. For a Church to qualify for Basilica status it must be of both historical and aesthetic significance. It's relevant that all Basilicas have their own unique Coat of Arms on which one item is held in common—the two Keys to the Kingdom of Heaven.

St. Lawrence: When it comes to bringing the Church into full stature St. Lawrence plays an important role. This is because he was a deacon of the Church who helped preserve the faith not only through his faithful and devout life, but also through the testimony of his martyrdom.

In the year 258, when the Church was being persecuted, the Prefect of Rome demanded Lawrence bring him the treasures of the Church. Lawrence returned with the sick and poor, rightfully claiming them to be the Church's treasures. Infuriated, the emperor condemned him to "burn" to death on an iron grill.

St. Lawrence's martyrdom by fire is a foreshadowing of the purification that must take place in the Church before it can be brought into completion and perfection. This is confirmed by St. Peter who tells us that before the New Heaven and New Earth can come the second heaven and earth must go through the following: *"...the elements shall be 'melted with heat' and the earth and works which are in it shall be burnt up [with the heat of salt]."* (2 Peter 3:10) St. Peter continues, *"Looking for and hastening unto the coming of the day of the Lord, by which the heavens being on fire shall be dissolved, and the elements shall melt with burning heat. But we look for new heavens, and a new earth according to His promises, in which justice dwelleth."* (2 Peter 3:12-13) These promises of God coincide with the Salt Covenant through which God promised David and his sons the Kingdom over Israel forever.

Then just one verse away St. Peter writes, *"And account the long-suffering of our Lord, salvation; as also our most dear brother Paul, according to the wisdom given him, hath written to you; As also in all his epistles, speaking in them of these things; in which are certain things hard to be understood, which the unlearned and unstable wrest, as they do also the other scriptures, to their own destruction."* (2 Peter 3:15-16) This longsuffering of the Lord which is hard to understand is that Jesus Christ truly continues to suffer in Christ Jesus who lives within God's people, and whose sufferings[93] are needed to bring the Mystical Body of Christ into full stature.

True Love for God and neighbor is what inspired and compelled St. Lawrence to ever so humbly lay down his life, uniting his sufferings with those of Jesus. The story's been passed down that St. Lawrence was even given the amazing grace to joke as he lay tied to the gridiron. Burning, he quipped, "Turn me over I'm done on this side!"

St. Lawrence's sacrificial death by fire brings to mind these words also found in St. Peter's second epistle, *"Dearly beloved, think not strange the burning heat which is to try you, as if some new thing happened to you; But if you partake of the sufferings of Christ, rejoice that when His glory shall be revealed, you may also be glad with exceeding joy."* (I Peter 4:14). Here again we see the cross as a prerequisite for sharing in God's Glory.

<u>The Coat of Arms</u>: The Basilica of St. Lawrence's Coat of Arms is pictured below. Note how it reflects the knowledge of the Gospel

---

93 There are some Christians who believe that suffering reveals a lack of faith in God's healing power. They often quote Jesus' words, *I have come that they may have life, and may have it more abundantly.* This abundant life is the everlasting life Jesus promises those who eat His Body and drink His Blood, as seen in John 6:48-59. Of course, just as Jesus healed on earth, He continues to heal on earth to show His saving power and grace. However, those whom He healed eventually succumb to death. Thus the greatest healing grace of all is when a soul turns to God and accepts his or her cross for the love and greater Glory of God.

of Christ's Glory being unveiled. For example, at top center you see the symbol of the dome. Under which are the two Keys to the Kingdom of Heaven, which represent God's substance of Glory and God's Name of Glory. To their left is the Eucharistic Host and Chalice, representing the Body and Blood of Jesus Christ. Directly below is seen the Crown of God's Glory suspended over the waters or sea of His Glory. To their far right is a grill, denoting the method by which St. Lawrence entered into glory, martyrdom by fire! The palm branch over the grill represents martyrdom. Finally, the mountains on the bottom not only represent the Blue Ridge Mountains where the Basilica of St. Lawrence is located, but also the emergence of Christ's rising Glory.

St. Raphael: On the wall behind the main altar of the Basilica there is a beautiful seven-foot terra cotta figure of the Archangel Raphael with two fish (Jesus Christ/Christ Jesus) in hand. St. Raphael is also beautifully depicted in a stained glass window in the Marian Chapel of the Basilica.

It is no coincidence that the builder and architect of the Basilica, Raphael Guastavino was named after the archangel Raphael. This is of relevance because we invoke the Archangel Raphael's intercession for cures—healing. Recall that it is through the Archangel

Raphael's intervention that Tobias was cured of blindness with a salted gallbladder of a fish—see the Book of Tobias 6:5-9.[94] It is also significant that the Archangel Raphael helped to arrange a lasting marriage for Tobias' son Tobit. Tobit who happened to be his wife Sarah's "seventh" husband. Her previous six husbands passed away on the night of their wedding ceremony before their marriage could be consummated..

Consequently, because St. Paul instructs us that "all" Scripture is meant for instruction and also that *"blindness in part has happened to Israel,"*[95] it follows that the same remedy that healed Tobias of blindness—a fish and salt—will also heal Israel of its blindness. The fish, being the ancient Christian symbol for Jesus Christ/Christ Jesus; and the salt being the substance of the Covenant God made with David and his sons, the Covenant through which God promised to give them the Kingdom over Israel forever.

This covenant is now being brought into perfection and completion through the knowledge of God's better and lasting substance of the promise—the salt in the precious Blood of Jesus—the sacrificial Lamb of God.

For this reason, just as a fish and salt were necessary to heal Tobias of blindness, so too is the knowledge of Jesus Christ/Christ Jesus and His sanctifying substance salt necessary to <u>lift the veil</u> of blindness from the eyes of the Israelites. Of this veil of blindness St. Paul writes: *"But their senses were made dull. For, until this present day, the selfsame **veil**, in the reading of the Old Testament, remaineth not taken away because in Christ it is made void."* (2 Corinthians 3:14)

Dear saints in Christ Jesus, in looking at the bigger picture we can now see how the veil over the eyes of the Israelites corresponds to

---

94 The Book of Tobias/Tobit is a part of the Greek Septuagint— one of "7" books our Protestant brethren removed from the Bible.
95 Romans 11:25

the veil the woman has placed over the three measures of meal—the three Persons in one God. The good news is that the woman, the Virgin of the Unveiling, is now lifting the veil and making known the leavening ingredient for their, as well as our, healing, *"For there is nothing hid that shall not be made manifest."*

Incidentally, it is also providential that Father Joachim's birth name was John Raphael. John representing God's beloved and Raphael representing Father Joachim's healing ministry.

The Basilica Domes: The beautiful dome the architect Raphael Guastavino built is significant because it is a symbol of the great and mighty dominion that God desires to restore on earth through the knowledge of salt rising from under its dome and forthcoming from under the Vatican Dome—the Basilica of St. Peter. (Father Joachim believed that the Church would proclaim the Gospel of Christ's Glory infallible.)

St. Francis (1184-1226) the Man of Peace: St. Francis, known by many throughout the world as the "Man of Peace," is a bridge that is helping all nations to unite. Like St. Francis, his Franciscan followers will play an important role in restoring peace to the Church and world.

The following events in world history testify to St. Francis' great role in bringing about world Peace. The first took place in October of 1996 when Saint, then Pope, John Paul II selected St. Francis' home town of Assisi for the historic "Peace" initiative in which 235 Christian and Non-Christian leaders from throughout the world gathered in Assisi for a "Day of Prayer for World Peace." The second event occurred when the editors of the secular "Time Magazine" ranked St. Francis the Greatest Man of the Second Millennium. The third event took place in Vatican City on October 26, 1999, when Pope, now Saint, John Paul II met with over 200 religious leaders, representing twenty different religions from throughout the world, to discuss and pray for World Peace—this event culminated in Assisi with prayer for peace and unity. Then again in Assisi on January 24, 2001 when our Holy Father Pope John Paul II called for all religious leaders, particularly Muslims and Christians to pray for world peace and unity. Next, during Pope Benedict XVI's pontificate when he too called forth a gathering of religious leaders to gather in Assisi to pray for unity and peace. This meeting took place in October 2011. And finally, our present Holy Father, who also works tirelessly for world peace and unity, has paid St. Francis the ultimate tribute by taking His name – Pope Francis.

St. Francis' great love was holy poverty which he referred to as Lady Poverty. He embraced her with perfect joy in true imitation of Christ. Our Holy Father Pope Francis has also embraced holy poverty – as is so often reflected in his lifestyle choices.

The message Saint Francis proclaimed to men and women far and near was "The Gospel of Peace." St. Francis heard God's words "RePAIR my house which has fallen into ruin." Franciscans are again being called in a special way, albeit this time, to ReNEW the house of the Lord—to bring it into perfection through the preaching of "The Gospel of the Glory of Christ" now being revealed.

Working on renewing the house of the Lord, Pope Francis went to Assisi on the Feast of St. Francis October 4, 2013. Here, in the very place where St. Francis stripped himself of his costly garments, Pope Francis exhorted the faithful to strip themselves of their wealth and worldly attachments.

St. Francis' role in bringing the Glory of God full circle is seen in the powerful Chaplet of the Holy Ghost. This chaplet was composed by a Franciscan Capuchin missionary in the year 1892, and approved by Pope Leo XIII in 1902. It is intended to be in regard to the Holy Ghost what the Dominican rosary is in regard to the Blessed Virgin Mary. This powerful chaplet is comprised of five mysteries commemorating the five wounds of Jesus. In each of these five meditations the "GLORY BE" is prayed "7" times.

The Church, Christ's Mystical Body

To construct a beautiful church on earth, like the Basilica, a precise blue-print is needed as well as the proper materials for the foundation and structure. It also takes time, planning, talent, treasure, supervision, and management to unify and bring it into completion.

Supernaturally these same requirements are necessary to construct and bring to completion God's eternal Church of Glory. The precise blue print is His written Word—the Bible. The proper materials for the Church's foundation and structure are the Body and Blood of Jesus Christ dispensed to us through, with and in the seven sacraments.

The Church's mystical construction (Christ's Mystical Body— the Mystery of Christ' Glory) has been taking place for the last 2000 years under the authority of the Pope and the management and supervision of the good priests and bishops of the One Holy Catholic and Apostolic Church.

1) The Church's foundation is built on:
    a) Sacred Scripture and
    b) Holy Tradition
2) The Church's structure is built with:
    a) The Proper Matter
    b) The Proper Form

An explanation on the importance of the Proper Matter and Form is forthcoming.

THE GOSPEL OF PEACE SHALOM

Listen to these beautiful words St. Paul speaks about the feet of those who preach the Gospel of Peace: *"How beautiful are the feet of them that preach the Gospel of Peace of them that bring 'tidings of good things."* (Romans 10:15)

These tidings of "good things" can be likened to:

- The *"holy things"* of David Faithful (Acts 13:34)
- The blessing *of "things to come"* which Isaiah gave his sons Jacob and Esau. (Romans 11:20)
- *"The things that were first* and *the new things"* God is making us hear before they are about to spring forth. (Isaiah 42:9)
- The *"great things"* the Lord has done unto Mary *"and Holy is His Name."* (Luke 1:49)
- The *"substance of things to be hoped for."* (Hebrews 11:1)
- The *"two immutable things"* God declared the oath by to the heirs of the promise. (Hebrew 6:18)
- *"Those things which are 'now' being declared to you."* (1 Peter 1:12-14)

These things are represented by the two Keys that open the doors to God's Kingdom over Israel forever. They are the substance of Christ's Glory and His Holy and Blessed Name of Glory.

<u>These keys that Jesus gave to Peter are traditionally depicted as two</u>. They will be shown to ultimately represent: 1) the Living Waters and Sanctifying Salt of our incorruption. 2) God's Holy and Blessed Name of Glory.

As you read the following keep in mind that because there is no time or space with God, He sees everything that has happened, is happening, and will happen, all at once. We, however, in time, compartmentalize these events into the three dimensions of past, present, and future.

This can be applied to Jesus' words *"Do not think that I came to destroy the law, or the prophets. I am not come to destroy, but to fulfill."* (Matthew 5:17) Jesus did not come to destroy the law or the prophets but to fulfill them, because:

* What happened in the **Temple**, <u>the past</u>, was **good**.
* What is happening in the **Catholic Church** – <u>the present</u>, is **better.**[96]
* What is happening in **Heaven** – <u>our future</u>, is **best**.

We will now examine the first key to the Kingdom of Heaven. This key opens the door to the use of water and salt in "the outer courts" of the three holy places—the Temple, the Catholic Church, and Heaven. Here we will glimpse the progression of water and salt from good, to better, to best

The Temple's Outer Court: In the outer court of the Temple was found what was called a "great bronze sea of laver, in which priests bathed before entering on their ministry."[97] There was also a special bowl of laver—salt and water—in which the High Priest washed his hands before entering the Holy of Holies.

---

96 Albeit, supernaturally, attending Mass is going to Heaven, the veil has just not been lifted.

97 <u>How Christians said the First Mass</u>, Father James L. Meagher, D.D. pg. 245.

<u>The Roman Catholic Church's Outer Court</u>: The Temple's sea of laver corresponds to the water and salt in the Holy Water fonts placed in Catholic churches of the Roman Rite at the doors of entry; this entryway would correspond to the Temple's outer court. Upon entering the church God's priestly people dip their fingers into the Holy Water and then make the Sign of the Cross on their person. This blessing, which helps us recall our Baptism, has traditionally been known to remit venial sin—in other words it helps to free the soul from corruption. Whereas the bowl the High Priest washed his hands in before entering the Holy of Holies would correspond to the bowl of salted water[98] the priests of the Roman Catholic Rite washed their hands in before the Consecration at Holy Mass. (Placing salt in this water is no longer a mandatory part of the liturgy.)

<u>Heaven's Outer Court</u>: The sea of glass like to crystal, *"And in the site of the throne was, as it were, a sea of glass like to crystal; and in the midst of the throne, and round about the throne, were four living creatures, full of eyes before and behind. (4:6). And the four living creatures had each of them six wings; and round about and within they are full of eyes. And they rested not day and night, saying: Holy, holy, holy, Lord God Almighty, who was [past], and who is [present], and who is to come [future]."* (4:8) Our Lord and Savior Jesus Christ, not only encompasses all things in Heaven and earth but all time as well.

---

98 Besides cleansing the hands this would also correspond to when Pontius Pilate publicly washed his hands before sentencing Jesus to crucifixion to show he would have no part in His death. In the same way Catholic Priests also wash their hands before sacrificing Jesus mystically to show they do not take part in the sacrifice.

In summary, the Key to God's Outer Court, water and salt, prepares us to enter into God's inner sanctuary by helping to cleanse us of our sins.

The Second Key to the Kingdom is to God's Inner Sanctuary: This most precious key brings us into the deepest intimacy we can possibly have with God—the great consummation of our marriage. It is through this key that we are able to enter into God's bosom— His Inner Sanctuary. Now we will glimpse its progression from good, to better and best.

In the Temple: this key corresponds to the Holy of Holies, within which the High Priest entered once a year on Yom Kippur to call upon the Lord's Sacred Name Yahweh (Creator/ Father/Spirit) and ask for His blessings, the first of which was for heavy rains. Yom Kippur is also known as the Day of Atonement because the High Priest offered animal sacrifice to atone for his sins and those of the people. Within the Holy of Holies was the Ark of the Covenant which meaningfully contained a "pot of manna/bread from Heaven;" as well as the Ten Commandments and the rod of Aaron. The High Priest had to pass through a veil to enter into the Holy of Holies.

In the Catholic Church: This key corresponds to the key to the Catholic Church's Tabernacle, which also veiled, contains the everlasting Bread of Life—Jesus Christ (Redeemer/Son/ Soul) our High Priest. Jesus, whose sacrifice, once for all, atones for the sins of all mankind. Everyday tens of thousands of Catholic Priests call upon the Sacred Name of the Lord as they offer the un-bloody Sacrifice of the Mass – showing the death of the Lord until he comes. This, the Pascal Mystery, is bringing into fulfillment the reign of Christ.

<u>In Heaven</u>: this key opens the door to "the New Jerusalem" (Sanctification/Spouse/Body) where the veil is now lifted. Here there is no longer any need for the sacrifice because the day of at-**one**-ment is fulfilled. Here we shall not only behold the everlasting Bread of Life—Jesus—we will reign with Him for all eternity. Through the full knowledge and understanding of this most powerful key, revealed in chapters IX through XII, we will come to invoke God's holy and blessed Name of Glory with all the praise and honor it is so deserving of. The knowledge of this key unlocks the door to God's inner sanctuary.

The above two keys enable us to enter into complete and perfect sacred unity of oneness with Christ and His Kingdom of Glory. Through this transforming knowledge we will come to put on "the new man" of which St. Paul writes, *"And <u>putting on the new</u>, him who is <u>renewed unto knowledge,</u> according to the image of Him who created him."* (Colossians 3:10)

The image of God in whose knowledge we are being renewed is that of His beginning substance, the living waters and sanctifying salt from the Light of His Sea of Glory. This knowledge isn't so hard to fathom when you consider that the two most vital components of our bodies are water and salt. God is truly an Ocean of Divine Mercy!

Through this transforming knowledge our eyes will be opened and our hearts enlarged. Then filled with wonder our conversion, a total turning to God, will come about: *"Then shalt thou see, and abound, and thy heart shall wonder and be enlarged, when <u>the multitude of the sea shall be converted to thee</u>, the strength of the Gentiles shall come to thee."* (Isaiah 60:5)

Dear saints, in the same way the Old Covenant Cloud of God's Glory led God's people, by day, into the Promise Land, so too is it now—through the Blood of Christ—leading God's people into the fulfillment of His promise—the New Jerusalem.

Before going any deeper, let us praise the Holy Trinity:

Abba Father, in your Divine Will, we love, adore, praise, thank and glorify you for keeping your promise of Truth, for it is written: *"The Lord hath sworn 'Truth to David' and he will not make it void: of the fruit of thy womb I will set upon thy throne. If thy children will keep my covenant [Salt Covenant] and these my testimonies which I shall teach them."* (Psalm 131:11-12)

Lord Jesus, in your Divine Will, we love, adore, praise, thank and glorify you for coming in excesses of love and profound humility and for sacrificing your life to fulfill the Salt Covenant God made with David and his sons to give them the Kingdom over Israel forever. This is the better and more lasting substance of the promise St. Paul mentions in Hebrews chapter 10 verses 34-36, because it is being fulfilled with the sanctifying substance salt in your precious Body and Blood.

Holy Spirit, in your Divine Will, we love, adore, praise, thank and glorify you for your gift of peace and unity and also the love you are pouring forth into us through the sanctifying seven sacraments and your seven gifts of knowledge, wisdom, courage, understanding, piety, counsel, and fear of the Lord. These glorious sacraments and gifts are now making known the very revelations of Jesus Christ that St. Paul was shown in the Third Heaven and is now unveiling to us through the scriptures.

CHAPTER 9

§

"Jesus did not reveal the Holy Spirit fully
until His death and resurrection when He has been glorified,
but little by little He alluded to Him
as when He said 'His own flesh' will be food
for the life of the world."

CATECHISM OF THE CATHOLIC CHURCH
SECTION 728

- The Holy Spirit - The Crowning of Jesus' Anointed Body Risen and Glorified.

§

Jesus' Anointed Body—Risen & Glorified

The Sacrifice of Unleavened Bread—tempered with oil: In Chapter 2 of the Book of Leviticus, God instructs His people how to make a bread sacrifice to the Lord, it is to be of fine flour without leaven and anointed with oil: *"But when thou offerest a sacrifice baked in the oven of flour, to wit, loaves without leaven, tempered with oil, and 'unleavened wafers, anointed with oil"* (vs.4); *"if thy oblation be from the frying pan, of flour tempered with oil, and without leaven thou shalt divide it into little pieces, and shall; 'pour oil upon it"* (vs.5-6); *"And if the sacrifice is from the gridiron, in like manner the flour shall be tempered with oil…"* (Vs.7)

First of all, this sacrifice of unleavened bread is a pre-figuration of Jesus' Body which was to become the sacrifice made new. This is why Jesus' Body in the Latin Rite is consecrated under the species of unleavened bread.

Secondly, the sacrifice was not to contain the leaven yeast—and this is because yeast is a fungus that lacks chlorophyll from the sun's light. Whereas, the rising of the Bread of Life—Jesus—was to come from the leaven Salt, from the Light of the Son!

Thirdly, is the understanding that the olive oil poured upon the unleavened bread is a pre-figuration of Jesus' anointed Body.

Lastly, the unleavened bread tempered with oil, baked in the oven and risen is a foreshadowing of Jesus, the Bread of Life, anointed, crucified and risen – the crowning love, substance and unity of the Holy Spirit!

It is not a coincidence that the Catechism of the Catholic Church, section 695, teaches that "the symbolism of anointing with oil signifies the Holy Spirit to the point of becoming a synonym for the Holy Spirit." And since the Catechism also teaches that the Third Divine Person of the Holy Trinity reveals in its fullness the mystery of the Blessed Trinity (see section 244) it makes sense that the Holy Spirit would mysteriously make visible the sacred substance that unites all three Divine Persons of the Holy Trinity.

The revelation of the love, substance and unity that resides in Jesus' anointed, risen and glorified Body is the Gospel of the Holy Ghost that St. Peter is instructing us to trust perfectly in:

> *"Searching what or what manner of time the Spirit of Christ in them did signify: when it foretold those sufferings that are in Christ, and the 'glories that should follow': To whom it was revealed, that not to themselves, 'but to you' they ministered 'those things' [water, salt, and oil – substance/unity] which are 'now declared,*[99] *to you by them that have* **PREACHED THE GOSPEL TO YOU, THE HOLY GHOST** *being sent down from Heaven on whom the angels desire to look. Wherefore having the loins of your mind girt up, being sober,* **TRUST PERFECTLY IN THE GRACE WHICH IS OFFERED YOU IN THE REVELATION OF JESUS CHRIST,** *as*

---

99 Recall in the Book of Isaiah how the Lord promised that before "the new things spring forth" he would "declare them?" He is "now", in what St. Paul refers to as "due time", declaring them.

children of obedience, not fashioned according to the former desires of your ignorance." (I Peter 1:11-14)

Chapter One of St. Peter's first epistle is all about the glories that follow Jesus' suffering and how we in this last time, <u>through His anointed,</u> <u>risen glorified Flesh,</u> will come to participate in the very life, suffering, death, and risen Glory of Christ. This is how we are to attain what St. Peter calls *"an inheritance incorruptible," "ready to be revealed in the last time," "Foreknown indeed before the foundation of the world, but manifested in the last time..."* (I Peter 1: 4, 5 & 20).

The preaching of the Gospel of the Holy Ghost, our incorruptible inheritance, now being manifested in the last time, is the grace that is necessary to bring about the unveiling of Jesus Christ and all of His Glory within us!

The Oil of the Olive

The olive tree and its fruit: Olive groves are a beautiful sight throughout the picturesque rolling hills of the Holy Land. These attractive groves glisten in the sun owing to the silver green leaves of the olive tree.

It's interesting that there is an olive grove on the Mount of Olives, where Jesus often went to pray and also where He agonized, in which scientists believe the trees are more than 2000 years old. It is also remarkable that olive trees seem to live forever. For example, even if fire consumes an olive grove, the roots of the olive trees will spring up producing anew. And yet, despite their resilient longevity, in order for olive trees to produce an abundance of good fruit they must be diligently pruned and cultivated.

The fruit of an olive tree flows forth from a cluster of small white blossoms. When ripened, the fruit—the green olive—changes color to violet, deep purple, and some to black. It's notable that if you were to pick and eat a ripe olive from a tree it would be far too bitter for edibility. To rectify this bitterness, the treatment of choice is putting the olives into concentrated brine, a solution of salt and water, for as long as six months.

Olive oil: Olive oil, a part of every-day cuisine in the Mediterranean, is not only rich in vitamins and minerals (particularly the anti-aging antioxidants A & E); it is the healthiest fat we can consume. Another one of the health benefits derived from consuming olive oil is that it helps to decrease bad (LDL) cholesterol in the blood and increase good (HDL) cholesterol. Olive oil is therefore linked to decreasing the risk for heart disease, arteriosclerosis and even cancer. Olive oil is also known for boasting the immune system's function.

Extra virgin oil is made from fresh picked ripe olives whose oil and water is pressed out. Since no heat is required this process is called first cold press. Other inferior variations of olive oil are called virgin, pure, and light. Olive oil, in any one of its variations, is also good for the skin's integrity, either consumed or applied topically.

Its worthy of note that fat is what provides the structural framework for all our body's cells. In fact, without fat we would be like a puddle – without shape or form! This is notable because the knowledge of the fat of the olive now being revealed is what will prove necessary to bring the Mystical Body of Christ (God's people) into "full structure/stature." Once again, God uses the knowledge of the natural to bring His supernatural plan into fulfillment!

Biblical History of Olive Oil: Throughout both the Old and New Covenant the olive plays a significant and profound role as seen in the following.

The olive tree has always been a symbol of new life, peace, and restoration. For instance, after the flood God sent to purify the earth, the first sign of new life springing forth from the earth was the olive tree as seen in Genesis Chapter 8: When Noah first sent forth the dove she returned not finding a place to rest. Then, after waiting seven days, he sent her forth again and this time she came back in the evening carrying a branch from an "olive tree" in her beak. It is for this reason that the dove – a symbol of the Holy Ghost – with an olive branch in her beak symbolizes the restoration of new life and peace on earth.[100]

The seven days Noah waited before sending out the dove again prefigures, among other things, the seven sacraments, administered throughout a period of time, in which the Holy Ghost is restoring new life and peace on earth.

The Glory of the Olive Tree: The significance of the olive tree as well as water and salt, is evidenced in the following scripture in which God is demonstrating His favor to the penitent: *"I will be 'as the dew,' Israel shall spring as the lily, and his root shall shoot forth as that*

---

100 It was revealed to Blessed Anne Catherine Emmerick, who was beatified in October 2004, that the only thing Adam and Eve were allowed to take with them from the Garden of Paradise was a branch from an olive tree.

of Libanus. His branches shall spread, and his glory shall be as 'the olive tree': and his smell as that of the Libanus." (Book of Osee/Hosea 14:6-7)

Note how God tells us the penitent's Glory will be as "the olive tree" thus connecting the Glory of God with the olive—the symbol of restoration, peace and new life; also note how He says He will be "as the dew," as in water and salt, a sign of refreshment and cleansing.

The Olive Tree, a Metaphor for the House of Israel: In the following excerpts from Romans Chapter 11, St. Paul metaphorically refers to the House of Israel as an Olive Tree. He then describes how the Gentiles are to be grafted into the natural Olive Tree: *"For I say to you, Gentiles: as long indeed as I am the apostle of the Gentiles, I will honor my ministry. If by any means, I may provoke to emulation them who are my flesh, and may save some of them. For if the loss of them be the reconciliation of the world, what shall the receiving of them be, but life from the dead? For if **the firstfruit** be holy, so is the lump also: and if the root be holy, so are the branches. And if some of the branches be broken, and thou, being a wild olive, art in-grafted in them, and art made partaker of the root, and of **the fatness of the olive tree,** boast not against the branches. But if thou boast, thou bearest not the root, but the root thee. Thou wilt say to them: The branches were broken off, that I might be grafted in. Well, because of unbelief they were broken off. But thou standest by faith: be not high minded, but fear. For if God hath not spared the natural branches, fear lest perhaps he also spare not thee. …And they also, if they abide not still in unbelief, shall be grafted in: for God is able to graft them in again. For if thou were cut out of the wild olive tree, which is natural to thee, and, contrary to nature, were grafted into **the good olive tree**; how much more shall they that are the natural branches, be grafted into their own olive tree?"*

How beautifully this parable upholds the profound meaning of olive oil when it comes to the grafting in of the Gentiles (the wild olive branch) into the House of Israel, and the re-grafting in of the Israelites (the natural olive branches) into the House of Israel.

This mystical metaphor clearly shows us the importance of the fruit of the olive tree when it comes to the restoration of the House of Israel. The House of Israel being an image of the Mystical Body of Christ whose structural framework, like our natural bodies, will be brought into full stature and splendorous glory through the knowledge of the fatness of the good olive tree.

Isaac's fatherly blessing: In Genesis Chapter 27:28-29, we read where Jacob, the second son of Isaac, tricked his father into giving him the blessing of the firstborn son. Esau, the firstborn, upon hearing this roared out with a great cry and with much consternation begged his father for a blessing too. Isaac being moved with pity then blessed Esau as well, bestowing on Esau the following portion of the blessing he bestowed on Jacob: *"In <u>the fat of the earth</u> and in <u>the dew of Heaven</u> from above shall your blessing be."*

This portion of the blessing Isaac bestowed on both his sons is so meaningful that St. Paul refers to it in Hebrew 11:20: ***"By faith also of things to come, Isaac blessed Jacob and Esau."*** (vs. 20). This blessing by faith "of things to come" is so important because these things to come are the ingredients, the composition, of Jacob and Esau's redeemed, sanctified and glorified bodies – as seen in the following:

* <u>The fat of the earth</u> – signifying the olive oil that will give structure/form to their redeemed and glorified new bodies. Esau and Isaac's bodies, as well as the bodies of the faithful departed, are still in the ground awaiting *"the redemption of our body, the firstfruits"* that St. Paul refers to in Romans 8:23.
* <u>The dew of Heaven</u> – represents the water and salt which has already given rise to Jacob and Esau's spirit and soul. As

they now exist they are a part of *"the cloud of witness"* St. Paul speaks about in Hebrews 12:1. (This gives insight into the manifestations of saints some people claim to see in cloud (water and salt) formation. The author once saw the 12 apostles, crystal clear, in cloud formation.)

Our Heavenly Father's Blessing: Just as the fatherly blessing that Isaac gave his sons consisted of water, salt and olive oil, so, too, does our heavenly Father's blessing consist of water, salt, and olive oil!

Our heavenly Father bestows His blessing on us through these very three elements in our Baptism. Baptism being the sacrament through which we are born again (restored) and rooted into God's family.

These three outward signs/symbols of inward grace—water, salt and olive oil—we receive through the sacrament of Baptism correspond to our perfect incorporation into the life of the Holy Trinity as follows:

1. The Water of Baptism—signifies the Father's Spirit.
2. The Salt in the Water of Baptism—signifies the Son's Soul.
3. The Olive Oil—signifies the Holy Spirit

It was for this reason that Jesus—in His risen and glorified Flesh— commanded the Apostles to go out and baptize all nations:

> In the Name of the Father (Spirit/ Water),
> And of the Son (Soul/Salt),
> And of the Holy Spirit (Body/Olive Oil).

Keeping in perspective the Catechism's teaching: "The symbolism of anointing with oil signifies the Holy Spirit to the point of becoming a synonym for the Holy Spirit." (Section 695)

The Redemption of our Body: In Romans chapter 8:22-23, St. Paul connects the first-fruits of the spirit, derived from the Good Olive Tree, with the redemption of the body when he writes: *"For we know that every creature groaneth and travaileth in pain, even until now. And not only it, but ourselves also, who have **the first-fruits of the Spirit**, even we ourselves groan within ourselves, waiting for the adoption of the sons of God, **the redemption of our body."***

In connecting the first-fruits of the Spirit with the redemption of our body, St. Paul seems to be making the point that the knowledge of the first-fruits is necessary to bring about the redemption of our body.

This is a good place to reflect on the present state of St. Paul's body which, along with the bodies of all the faithful departed, is still in the ground awaiting the redemption of the Body, Jesus' Coming in Glory. Remember that it isn't until the Coming of the Lord Jesus Christ that St. Paul's spirit and soul, as well as those of all the faithful departed, will be joined "whole" to his redeemed body!

This wholeness, as in holiness, is reflected in St. Paul's prayer for our sanctification: *"And may the God of peace Himself sanctify you in 'all things'; that your 'whole' spirit [water], and soul [salt], and body [olive oil], may be preserved blameless in the coming of our Lord Jesus Christ."* (I Thessalonians 5:23).

Priests were anointed with Olive Oil in the Old Salt Covenant—and so too in the Salt Covenant Made new: In the following Old Covenant Book of Exodus the Lord is giving Moses instruction on the manner of consecrating Aaron and other priests which necessarily involves pouring the oil of unction on his head: *"And thou shalt also do this, that they may be consecrated to me in priesthood. Take a calf from the herd, and two rams without blemish and unleavened bread, and a cake without leaven, tempered with oil, wafers also unleavened anointed with oil: thou shalt make them all of wheaten flour. And thou shalt bring*

Aaron and his sons to the door of the tabernacle of the testimony. And when thou hast washed the father and his sons with water, thou shalt clothe Aaron with his vestments, that I, with the linen garment and the tunic, and the ephod and the rational, which thou shalt gird with the girdle. And thou shalt put the mitre upon his head, and the holy plate upon the mitre, and thou shalt pour the oil of unction upon his head; and by this rite shall he be consecrated." (29: 1-7)

Here St. Paul's explains the office of a high priest in the New Covenant: *"For every 'high priest' taken from among men, is ordained for men in* <u>*the things*</u> *[water, salt and oil] that appertain to God, that he may offer up gifts and sacrifices for sins. Neither doth any man take the honor to himself, but he that is called by God, as Aaron was. So Christ also did not glorify himself that he might be made a high priest: but he that said unto him: thou are my Son, this day have I begotten thee. As he saith also in another place: 'Thou art a priest for ever, according to the order of Melchizedech."* (Hebrews 5:1; 3-6) For this reason the office of a High Priest in the New Salt Covenant follows the same method of consecration God commanded Moses to follow in the Old Salt Covenant, which includes an anointing with holy chrism (olive oil & balm).

In regards to the holy anointing of priests, the <u>Catechism of the Catholic Church</u> states that **"oil"** is **"a sign of the special anointing of the Holy Spirit who makes their ministry fruitful."** (CCC section 1574, bold added) Testifying once again to the specific relationship the "fruit of the olive" has with the Holy Spirit.

(Of the many miracles that have taken place in the home of Audrey Santos [1983-2007], the little victim soul from Worcester, Massachusetts, one is the appearance of oil that has filled, on many occasions, the ciborium and/or chalice during the Holy Sacrifice of the Mass—at which time the priest announces Holy Communion must be received on the tongue. Subsequently, at her Bishop's request, this oil was tested by a reputable laboratory and found to be comprised of olive oil! This oil from Heaven also exudes from many other holy objects in Audrey's home. The author has been there on many occasions – Heaven's outpouring of God's Glory at this humble site is truly magnificent to behold – pray for the grace to make a pilgrimage there.)

<u>The Mount of Olives</u>: In the Old Covenant the Mount of Olives is first mentioned in 2 King's/Samuel 15:30. Here David, like Jesus, ascends the Mount of Olives lamenting and weeping.

We also see in Zachariah Chapter 14 where the Lord's coming with all the saints (when we too shall be caught up with Him) is to take place on the Mount of Olives. This clearly points to the vital role the fruit of the olive tree will play in the restoration of all things!

Then in the New Covenant, we see Jesus sitting on the Mount of Olives where He is preaching the sign of His coming and of the consummation of the world: *"And while He was sitting on Mount Olivet, the disciples came to Him privately saying: Tell us when shall these things be? And what shall be the sign of thy coming, and of the consummation of the world?"* (Matthew 24:3)

The fact that Jesus was sitting on the Mount of Olivet when the disciples asked this question, is yet another clear sign of the importance of the fruit of the olive tree in bringing about the Coming of Christ and the consummation of the world.

It is also significant that it was from the Mount of Olives that Jesus, riding on an ass, descended to make His grand entry into Jerusalem. Five days later He would return to the Mount of Olives to begin His passion. This scene of Jesus' agony on the Mount of Olives depicts how the extraordinary treasures of the world are to be found hidden within the ordinary matter of things. For example, in Jesus' humanity not only was the sanctifying Dew from Heaven hidden, but also the redemptive Olive Oil of Gladness. This Olive Oil would three days later give structure/form to His Risen Body of Glory—the Crowning work of the Holy Ghost.

Gethsemane: The olive garden on the Mount of Olives where Jesus agonized over the sins of the world is called Gethsemane, which in Hebrew means "olive press." This is interesting because it was in this garden that Jesus' Passion began, when He took upon Himself the unfathomable burden, stretching over all time, of the sins of humanity. The intensity of His suffering was so extreme it caused Him to sweat blood.

The Blood Jesus sweat in the Garden of Olives, like the Blood of His Cross, contains our perpetual and everlasting blessing *of "things to come"* which, like the blessing Isaac gave his sons Jacob and Esau, is of the "dew of Heaven" and the "fat of the earth."

It's noteworthy that olive oil must be beaten and pressed to become pure. This is a similitude for the trials and tribulations our natural bodies, like Jesus', must undergo to become the pure and worthy living tabernacles of His Light. Our Light, unlike the light that burns outside the veil of the Tabernacle, is to burn perpetually, with pure and everlasting love, in complete unity with the Lord's.

The fruit from a tree in the Garden of Eden brought about the fall of mankind—as opposed to the fruit from a tree in the Garden of Olives which brings about mankind's sanctification: In humble and loving obedience to His Father's Will, Jesus' Passion began in a garden. This took place to counteract the disobedient and prideful act Adam and Eve committed in a garden. Their willful act, which took place through the jealous and hateful seduction of Lucifer, cast them out of the Light of God's Divine Will.

Here it is good to ponder how it was the fruit from a tree that brought about the fall of mankind, this is remarkable because it is also a fruit from a tree that is to sanctify and restore mankind—albeit a most bitter fruit—the fruit of the olive. Bear in mind how nature's bitter olive is made edible through soaking it in a brine of salt and water. Comparably, the bitterness of the supernatural olive is also made edible through salt and water—the very sanctifying salt and water in the precious Blood Jesus sweat in the Garden of Olives!

(Adam and Eve reached out their hands and grasped the forbidden fruit, whereas Jesus' hands were nailed to a fruit tree! There are scholars who believe Jesus was crucified on an olive tree.)

Oil in the New Salt Covenant is used to restore health to the spiritually and physically ill: In Mark 6:13 we read: *"And they cast out many devils, and anointed with oil many that were sick, and healed them."* Then in James 5:14 it is recorded: *"Is any man sick among you? Let him bring in the priests of the church, and let them pray over him, anointing him with oil in the Name of the Lord."*

Another example of olive oil being used for healing is seen in Luke chapter 10:30-35. Here Jesus tells the parable about the Good Samaritan who poured oil and wine into the wound of the victim of robbery. This parable can be interpreted as Jesus being the Good Samaritan who has paid the price for our healing, we are the victims robbed by Satan. The oil (of unction/salve) and wine (transformed into His precious Blood) would represent our sacramental journey that brings about our healing of spirit, soul and body.

The Penitent Cleanses and Anoints Jesus' Feet: In Luke Chapter 7:36-50, we see where Jesus is eating at the house of a Pharisee, whereat a penitent woman enters and begins to wash Jesus' feet with her tears and wipe them with the hairs of her head—she also kisses His feet and anoints them with precious ointment.

Then because Jesus allows this demonstration of love and humility by a sinner, the Pharisee doubts Him to be a prophet. Reading the Pharisee's mind, Jesus states: *"Dost thou see this woman? I entered into thy house, thou gavest me no water for my feet; but she with tears hath washed my feet, and with her hairs hath wiped them. Thou gave me no kiss; but she, since she came in, hath not ceased to kiss my feet. My head with oil thou dist not anoint; but she with ointment hath anointed my feet."* (vs.44-46)

The Pharisee was apparently too proud to honor Jesus with the "proper ritual." Yet the penitent who loved Jesus bowed down in humility then washing His feet with her tears (salt and water) she kissed them and anointed them with precious ointment, which likely contained virgin olive oil.

When you think about it, the penitent sought and found Jesus, the fullness of Truth, to whom she submitted with love and humility. In this same way Jesus' Mystical Body on earth, the Catholic Church, like Jesus Himself, also contains the fullness of Truth.

Therefore, those who, like the penitent, bow in humble submission to the Church's Magisterium, return to God all the honor and glory He so richly deserves.

<u>The Parable of the Ten Virgins</u>: In Matthew 25:1-12 Jesus describes the Kingdom of Heaven to be like: *"ten virgins who taking their lamps went out to meet the bridegroom [Jesus] and the bride [His Church]. And five of them were foolish and five wise. But the five foolish having taken their lamps, did not take oil with them. But the wise took oil in their vessels with the lamps. And the bridegroom tarrying, they all slumbered and slept. And at midnight there was a cry made: Behold the bridegroom cometh, go ye forth to meet him. Then all those virgins arose and trimmed their lamps. And the foolish said to the wise: 'Give us of your oil, for our lamps are gone out. The wise answered, saying: Lest perhaps there be not enough for us and for you, go ye rather to them that sell, and*

buy for ourselves. Now whilst they went to buy, the bridegroom came: and they that were ready, went in with him to the marriage, 'and the door was shut.' But at last came also the other virgins, saying: Lord, Lord open to us. But he answering said: 'Amen, I say to you, I know you not.

In pondering these verses, first think about how the door to the wedding feast was shut to the virgins without oil. Next, recall how Jesus gave Peter the key to both open and shut the door to the Marriage Feast. Now consider how this very key to the Marriage Feast, a metaphor for the Kingdom of Heaven, has been handed down in succession to the Popes of the Catholic Church. This is important to understand because the Church mandates that one of the forms of matter in our sacramental journey to Heaven's Marriage Feast be olive oil.

For example, oil is used to anoint God's priestly people in the following sacraments: 1) Baptism 2) Confirmation 3) Holy Orders 4) and the Anointing of the Sick, which is often times administered to us on our final journey to Heaven).

Thus, it could be said that in their journey to the Wedding Feast the five wise virgin's received "the proper anointing" of the Holy Spirit–with the Chrism Oil which contains virgin olive oil, whereas the five foolish virgins did not seek to be properly anointed.

You could also say that the five foolish virgins, who took their lamps but had no olive oil, were not properly dressed because they did not, nor will not accept the knowledge of the sanctifying work of the Holy Spirit, whose full knowledge is now being made known.

The Two Olive Trees

The Old Covenant speaks of the Two Olive Trees in Chapter 4 of the Book of Zachariah: Here, in a vision, Zachariah sees a golden candlestick upon which are the seven lights and seven funnels for the lights, over which are *the two Olive Trees*—one on the right side and one on the left.

When Zachariah inquires to the Lord about these seven lights, the Lord responds: *"These are the seven eyes of the Lord, that run to and from through the whole earth."* These seven eyes of the Lord, besides representing the seven sacraments, represent the seven gifts of the Holy Spirit. These gifts of knowledge, wisdom, counsel, courage, understanding, piety and fear of the Lord, spring forth from the seven sacraments.

When Zachariah inquires further as to who *"are **the two olive branches**, that are **the two golden beaks**, in which are the funnels of gold?"* The Lord God of hosts responds: *"These are **the two sons of oil** who stand before the Lord of the whole earth."* (4:14)

First of all, these "two olive branches" correspond to St. Paul's parable mentioned earlier in which he mystically refers to the House of Israel as an Olive Tree. Recall how St. Paul compares the natural olive branch with the Israelites and the olive branch that is grafted in with the Gentiles. This metaphor therefore suggests that one of the two olive branches in Zachariah's vision would be a prophet of natural Jewish origin—most likely Elias/Elijah, according to most of the Church Fathers. Whereas, the other olive branch would be a prophet of non-Jewish origin, most likely Enoch who, like Elias/ Elijah, walked with God and was taken up from the earth without seeing death.

Secondly, the two prophets are described as having *"golden beaks"* which takes us back to the Book of Genesis wherein we saw Noah releasing the dove for the second time whereupon the dove, a symbol for the Holy Spirit, returns with an *"olive branch"* in her *"beak."* The dove and the olive branch have ever since symbolized new life, peace, and restoration—the very new life, peace, and restoration that the preaching of the Gospel of the Holy Ghost is to bring about.

The golden beaks would therefore be analogous to the preaching, by the two sons of oil, of the knowledge of the Holy Ghost—synonymous with the golden virgin olive oil—whose wisdom and understanding thereof is the gift that will bring the Mystical Body of Christ into full stature.

Thirdly, the two olive branches in Zachariah's vision are called "the two sons of oil" because they are the sons of the finest and purest golden virgin olive oil—from the Tree of Life (Genesis 2:9). <u>The Tree of Life which will prove to be that of the Olive!</u>

The New Covenant speaks of the Two Olive Trees and their Testimony in Chapter 11 of the Book of Revelation: Here St. John describes Two Olive Trees who go around the world prophesying for one thousand two hundred and sixty days (3 ½ years) in sackcloth. During this time, they are given great power *"even to shut Heaven; that it rain not in the days of their prophecy: and they have power over waters to turn them into blood, and to strike the earth with all plagues as often as they will. 'And when they shall have finished their testimony,' the beast, that hath ascendeth out of the abyss, shall make war against them, and shall overcome them, and kill them."* (vs. 6-7)

Their dead bodies are to lie in the streets of the great city, where their Lord also was crucified, for 3 ½ days for the entire world to see[101]. *"And after three days and a half, the spirit of life from God entered into them. And they stood upon their feet, and great fear fell upon them that saw them. And they heard a great voice from heaven, saying to them: come up hither. And they went up to heaven in a cloud: and their enemies saw them (vs. 11).* Three verses later we read: *And the 'seventh' angel*

---

101 The Book of Revelation was written 2000 years ago when there was no such thing as television that would make it possible for the whole world to see the two olive tree witnesses lying dead!

sounded the trumpet: and there were great voices in heaven, saying: The Kingdom of this world is become our Lord's and His Christ's, and He shall reign forever and ever. Amen." (Rev. 11:15)

Chapter 10 of the book of Revelation provides even deeper insight into the testimony the Two Olive Trees are to give. Here St. John is instructed by the mighty angel, *"who standeth upon the sea [salt and water] and upon the earth [the fat of the earth],"* to go and take *"a little book"* that is *"open"* and *"eat it"*—the book we are told is sweet in his mouth and bitter in his stomach.

It is important to connect this little book with the Two Olive Trees because its content contains *"the testimony"* of Jesus' "anointed", risen and glorified Flesh to which these Two Olive Trees are to give witness. This is why both the knowledge in *"the little book open"* and *"the testimony the Olive Trees give"* indicate bringing about the Coming of the Lord, as evidenced in the following:

In Chapter 10 of the Book of Revelation the preaching of the prophetic knowledge contained in *"the little book open"*—to the many nations, and peoples, and tongues, and kings—is followed by the *"seventh"*[102] angel sounding the trumpet and *"the mystery of God is finished."* (vs. 10:7) In other words, the Kingdom of the Lord and His Christ's (Anointed) has come.

Then in Chapter 11 of Revelation when the Two Olive Tree witnesses have finished giving their testimony the seventh angel is also sounding his trumpet and *"the Kingdom of this world is become our Lord's and His Christ's [His Anointed] and He shall reign forever and ever. Amen."* In other words, the mystery of God is finished—all has been revealed—His Kingdom comes!

---

102 The "7th" angel is Gabriel—the archangel of Revelation and also of the Gentiles.

The Little Book Open: Bear in mind that when the Virgin of the Revelation appeared to the seer Bruno at Three Fountains, Rome, she held in her hands, clutched to her breast, a little book closed. This little closed book—the Book of Revelation/Unveiling has now been mystically opened by the suffering and death of *"the Lamb"* who is *"standing"* in the *"midst"* of the throne as though *"slain"* as seen in Revelation 5:6.

Also keep in mind that St. John the Beloved wrote the Book of Revelation while taken into the future: Thus he was seeing the Lamb, Jesus the Son of God, in complete unity of oneness with God's beloved Priest Sons.[103] These sons of God standing in the midst of the throne, offer the Holy Sacrifice of the Mass showing the death (as though slain) of the Lamb of God until He comes![104]

(Jesus Christ/Christ Jesus: In the following excerpt from Father Peter Klos' book <u>The Lady of All Nations Who Once was Mary</u> the visionary of this apparition site is describing a Sacred Host: "The host seemed to be made of fire. In the center of it was a little opening of depth. I cannot describe it any better. Then, all of a sudden, the host seemed to burst open and exposed to my view was a figure, soaring in mid-air, a person, exceedingly might and strong... I saw one person, but the thought kept recurring in my mind, 'and yet there are two;' and then when I looked I saw only one. Still my mind

---

103 Brides of the Most Blessed Trinity is a blessed apostolate who offer daily sacrifices for the Catholic priesthood. Go to www.bmbtnow.com to learn more

104 Like our Jewish brethren, who at Passover, were set free by partaking of an unblemished lamb, so too are we set free by partaking of Jesus—the unblemished Lamb of God—in Holy Communion. This, dear saints, is the Pascal Mystery – the mystery of the Lamb. Please contemplate the fact that at this present moment in time thousands of consecrated/anointed priests, celebrating Mass throughout the universal world, are showing the death of Our Jesus Christ until He comes again, as seen I Corinthians 11:24-29. Does this mean Catholics believe the priest is re-crucifying Christ? Absolutely not! But what it does mean is that the same sacrifice of Jesus' cross is made present to us at every Holy Mass. This is possible because there is no time or space with God. In other words, Jesus then could see and be with us now.

kept repeating 'and yet there are two.' All at once there came from the two an indescribable light and in it I saw, breaking out from the center- I cannot express it otherwise- a dove." Pg. 78)

<u>The Virgin's Virgin Olive Oil</u>:   All of the above considered, we are able to conclude that the Crowning work of the Holy Spirit would necessarily correspond with the knowledge, wisdom and understanding of virgin olive oil. However, not just any virgin olive oil—but the clearest, purest, and finest virgin olive oil, which, dear saints, will prove to be that of THE IMMACULATE VIRGIN MARY'S VIRGIN OLIVE OIL!

Yes! The Immaculate Virgin Mary is the Olive Tree of Life to whom the "two sons of oil" will give witness!!!

Now, is this saying the Virgin Mary is the Holy Spirit?   Of course not! However, it does mean that She and her Spouse are "one" in Sacred Unity—just as are all married couples one in sacred unity. The power in their most Loving and Sacred Unity is elaborated on in the next chapter.

To further validate the unveiling of this extraordinary revelation, the Virgin Mary appeared in Three Fountains, Rome, under the title "The Virgin of the Revelation" wearing an "OLIVE GREEN MANTLE!"

The Composition of the Mystical Body of Christ—our redeemed, sanctified and glorified body: As we have seen over and over again, God uses the natural to reveal the supernatural – the visible to reveal the invisible. Such is also the case for our glorified bodies, as seen in the following:

* **Water:** As we now exist our bodies are largely made up of water—approximately 55 to 75% water. Similarly, our

glorified bodies will be comprised of our Heavenly Father's life-giving Water.

* **Salt:** Salt is necessary for the human body to live, move, and have being. As will our glorified bodies live, move and have their being from salt – the Salt of the New Covenant promise. This sanctifying substance salt is found in the Precious Body and Blood of Jesus Christ dispensed to us in fullness through the seven sacraments of the One Holy Catholic and Apostolic Church.

* **Virgin Olive Oil:** Fat, which makes up our cell's structural framework, is what gives form to our human bodies. Correspondingly, our anointing with the fruit of the olive gives form to the total divinization of our redeemed and glorified bodies by the Holy Spirit.

Through this knowledge the Mystical Body of Christ will rise up in Glory into full splendor and stature.

Of God's great Glory soon to be revealed in us, St. Paul writes: *"For I reckon that the sufferings of this life are not worthy to be compared with the Glory to come, that shall be revealed in us!"* (Romans 8:18)

Brothers and sisters in Christ Jesus, we are now able to comprehend why virgin olive oil as well as tears of water and salt, are exuding from statues and other holy objects around the world: All of creation is crying out—anxious for the sons of God to be unveiled and revealed—anxious for the redemption of our bodies which soon follows.

CHAPTER 10

§

"Now what wisdom is, and what was her origin, I will declare:
and I will not hide from you 'the Mysteries of God,'
but will seek 'her' out from the beginning of 'her' birth,
and bring the Knowledge of 'her' to light,
and will not pass over the Truth."

THE BOOK OF WISDOM 6:24

The Olive Tree Lady Wisdom
The Woman of The Revelation

§

WHEN GOD'S LOVE SPOKE CREATION into being, He saw the whole of creation laid out before Him—the beginning, means, and end of all things.

Consequently, from the beginning He knew Lucifer would fall from grace and take one third of the angels to hell with him and He also knew that Adam and Eve, whom He would make in His own image and likeness, would also fall from grace and that a certain number of human beings would also follow to choose the path to hell.

The good news is that through His mercy, love, and goodness God has given mankind a second chance[105] to make restitution. This is why He established His law on the earth. However, God foresaw that His Law would not be enough to save mankind. Therefore, His Son, who was to become incarnate and whose principal mission on earth was to exalt and glorify His Father's Sacred Name, would now be asked to redeem the generations through His passion and death on a cross. This most merciful act of God's Son was needed to satisfy God's justice.

Now, if God, who reveals the invisible (supernatural) through the visible (natural), planned to have a son then God would first need a

---

105 The fallen angels choose to remain hateful.

spouse, would He not? And if God knew us before He formed us in the womb, as evidenced in Jeremiah 1:5, then certainly He knew His beloved spouse before He formed Her in the womb.

God's Spouse, Lady Wisdom

The Christians of the early Church recognized that King Solomon, who was given the knowledge and understanding of times past, present and future (as seen in Wisdom 7:18) was writing about God's Spouse in the following verses of the Book of Wisdom: *"Now what **wisdom** is, and what was **her origin**, I will declare: and I will not hide from you **the mysteries of God** but will seek her out from the beginning of her birth, and bring the knowledge of her to light, and will not pass over the <u>truth</u> (6:24). For she is an infinite treasure [full of grace] of men and I knew not that she was the mother of them all."* (7:12) If God is the Father of all, it makes sense that His Spouse is the Mother of all, would it not?

The Book of Wisdom continues, *"For she is more beautiful than the sun, and above all the order of the stars: being compared with the light, she is found before it."* (7:29); *"Her have I loved, and have sought her out from my youth, and have desired to take her for my spouse, and I became a lover of her beauty. She glorifieth her nobility by being conversant with God: yea and the Lord of all things hath loved her."* (8:2-3); *"Give me wisdom, that sitteth by thy throne [the spouse of the King sits by His throne] and cast me not from among thy children: For I am thy servant, and the son of thy handmaid…"* (9:4-5).

It is no coincidence that several times in the New Covenant the Virgin Mother of Jesus refers to herself as the handmaid of the Lord. As seen when the archangel Gabriel appeared to the Blessed Mother to announce that she was to be the Mother of Jesus, the son of God, and she responded: *"Behold the handmaid of the Lord be it done unto me according to your word."* (Luke 1:38)

The Book of Wisdom Chapters 6 through 10 speaks most particularly of God's spouse, Lady Wisdom.

<u>The Lord possessed Lady Wisdom before He made anything from the beginning</u>: In the Book of Proverbs Lady Wisdom is speaking at the gate of the city—the New Jerusalem. Listen with your hearts: *"For my fruit[106] is better than gold and precious stone, and my blossoms than choice silver."* (8:19) *"The Lord possessed me from the beginning of His ways, before He made anything from the [107]beginning I was set up from eternity, and of old before the earth was made. The depths were not as yet, and I was already conceived, neither had the fountains of water as yet sprung out."* (8:22-24) *"I was with him forming all things: and was delighted every day, playing before him at all times."* (Vs. 8:30)

First of all, as we reflect on the above, we know the *"fruit"* that is *"better than gold and precious stone"* is Jesus—the blessed fruit of Mary's womb. Secondly, the Lord possessed her from the beginning as would any spouse want his beloved with him as he set up home and garden.[108]

---

106 When Elizabeth, who was pregnant with John the Baptist, greeted Mary, who was pregnant with Jesus, Elizabeth cried out with a loud voice and said: *Blessed are thou among woman and <u>blessed is the fruit of thy womb</u>.* (Luke 1:42)

107 Eve was the first woman in the natural order – the Immaculate Virgin Mary, God's spouse, is the first woman in the supernatural order.

108 Our Jewish elders have a teaching that when God made Adam, He made him in His image and likeness – whole and complete. Then when God saw that it was not good for Adam to be alone He withdrew Eve from Adam's side – taking from Adam and giving to Eve feminine characteristics, i.e. gentleness, gracefulness, intuition, a heart for nurturing, etc.; leaving Adam with the more masculine characteristics, i.e. strength, leadership, agility, a heart for provision. This way Adam and Eve were to complete, complement, each other. Dear friends, in this same way, God's Immaculate Spouse Mary, who came forth from within God in the beginning complements Him. And again, in this same way Jesus' Bride, the Church, came forth from His side, His pierced Heart, and complements/completes Him!)

These beautiful words of Lady Wisdom are in the Bible because God so desires we come to know, love and honor His most beautiful, most pure, and most holy Spouse as He does. We'll come back to this enlightening chapter in the Book of Proverbs.

The Serpent's Jealousy of God's Love for the Woman: Mystics of the Church have long revealed that Lucifer's fall from grace came about when God in the beginning showed all the angels His plan of creation, which included His predilection for "the woman" who was to conceive His only begotten Son. According to St. Maximilian Kolbe, it was at this instant in time that Lucifer, the most brilliant angel, became jealous of "the woman" because he wanted this most elevated honor for himself. "After all," Lucifer thought, "I am the most beautiful and intelligent angel of all—what is mere man?" Lucifer's pride possessed him, and giving way to envy and hatred, he cunningly convinced one third of the angels to follow him in battle against God, the Woman, and her seed (Gen. 3:15).

You should know that Lucifer did not have a problem with loving and serving God. According to St. Maximilian Kolbe, it was his envy and jealousy of "the Woman" whom God elevated above him that enraged him. You should also know that it was because of God's love for the Woman—the mother of all the living—that mankind was given a second chance. However, it is not to be without difficulty because Lucifer and his cohorts are allowed, for a time, to tempt and ensnare us as they did Adam and Eve.

<u>Lady Wisdom and the Fruit of Her Womb, Jesus:</u> The Catholic Church has always honored and venerated the woman Mary as the Mother of God. In part because of these powerful words Elizabeth *"cried out in a loud voice to Mary—Blessed art thou among women, and blessed is the fruit of thy womb. And whence is this to me that the mother of my Lord should come to me? For behold as soon as the voice of*

thy salutation sounded in my ears, the infant in my womb leaped for joy." (Luke 1:42-44).

If you think about it, the Mother of Jesus was our Lord's living Tabernacle because just as David leaped when "the Ark of the Covenant," which contained the "manna/bread from Heaven," was brought before him, so too does St. John the Baptist leap in his mother's womb when "Mary," whose womb contains "the Bread of Eternal Life," is brought before him!

The Woman's Mission: Another reason the Catholic Church honors and venerates the Mother of Our Lord Jesus is found at what transpired at the wedding feast of Cana when Mary said to Jesus: *"They have no wine, and Jesus responded: 'Woman', what is that to me and to thee? My hour is not yet come. His mother then said to the waiters: Whatsoever He shall say to you, do ye,"* whereupon Jesus asked the waiters to fill the water pots with water (John 2:3-4). Here it is good to ponder that Jesus even as an adult was obedient to His mother. It is also significant that it was through His mother's request that Jesus changed the water into wine, whereby, as written in John 2:11, *He manifested His Glory.* And it was then that His public life began.

Jesus addressed His beloved mother in public formally as woman to publicly declare that She is "the woman" of whom His Father spoke in Genesis 3:15 when His Father said to the serpent: *"I will put enmities between thee and 'the woman' and thy seed and her seed; she shall crush thy head, and thou shalt lie in wait for her heel."* Jesus is of "her seed." whom He publicly addressed "woman!" This is why, as will be further substantiated, she is the woman who shall crush the head of the serpent!

So you see, just as Mary launched Jesus' public life at the wedding feast of Cana, so too did Jesus launch and make public His Mother's mission—to crush the head of the serpent. It is notable that this wedding scene was a foreshadowing of the Last Supper whereat Jesus, who is now the Bridegroom, turns the wine into His Blood.

Mary crushes the head of the serpent through her humility and obedience—the very two virtues opposed to the vices of pride and disobedience through which Adam and Eve succumbed to temptation. Pride: the serpent said to Eve you shall be as god's knowing good and evil. Disobedience: they ate "the forbidden fruit" (Genesis 3:6). And here's the scripture which reveals that it was through Mary's profound humility that the Word of God was able to become flesh in her womb: *"Because He hath regarded the 'humility' of His handmaid; for behold from henceforth all generations shall call me blessed."* (St. Luke 1:48). And here is the scripture that reveals the power in her obedience to God's Will: *"Behold the handmaid of the Lord be it done to me according to thy word."* (St. Luke 1:38)

Another profound scripture that confirms the woman Mary's important role in the salvation of mankind is demonstrated by these powerful words Jesus spoke to her from the cross: *"Woman, behold thy Son."* It is no coincidence that Jesus has once again addressed His beloved mother by the word "woman!" Next He speaks to His beloved Apostle John: *"Son, behold thy mother."* (St. John 19:26-7) First consider that at this most earth-shattering time in the history of mankind every word Jesus manages to utter, which causes Him agonizing pain beyond our comprehension, is of eternal significance! Thus, in once again publicly addressing His mother "woman," He is not only giving her to John as a spiritual mother but to all His beloved children. (In Matthew 27:56, we see that St. John the beloved's biological mother, the mother of the sons of Zebedee, was present at the scene of crucifixion.)

Jesus bequeathed Our Lady to us from the cross as our spiritual mother—we, like Jesus, are of "her seed." Please pray to understand that the serpent's cunning strategy is to diminish the role of "the woman" who is to crush his head—as well as to attack her seed—the Church—who honors and venerates Her. (Please, please pray fervently for our holy priests, they are in the front line of this most cunning and vicious attack.)

The Sign and Her Seed: In St. John the beloved's Book of Revelation Chapter 12, he makes reference to the woman "seven" times. In verse one he refers to her as "a woman" —the other references are recorded as "the woman": *"And a great sign[109] appeared in heaven: A woman clothed with the sun, and the moon under her feet, and on her head a crown of twelve stars: And being with child, she cried travailing in birth, and was in pain to be delivered." (vs.1-2)* This chapter significantly ends: *"And the dragon was angry against the woman: and went to make war with the rest of her seed, who keep the commandments of God, and have the testimony of Jesus Christ." (vs.17)*

The Woman St. John is yet again referring to, this time as a pregnant mother travailing in pain and about to give birth is as we've seen:

* The same woman God said would crush the head of the serpent.
* The same woman who gave birth to Jesus' First Coming.
* The same woman Elizabeth called *"blessed among all women"* and referred to as *"the mother of my Lord."*

---

109 Several visionaries have spoken about a great sign that is to appear in the sky at the time of a great illumination when we shall see ourselves as God sees us. In the book The City of God by the Venerable Mary of Agreda, it states that in the beginning the angels were all shown the great sign of the Virgin Mary pregnant with Jesus and that it was then that Lucifer proclaimed "I will not serve"! Taking into consideration that the things that shall be have already been, then the great sign at the time of the illumination could possibly be the Virgin Mary pregnant with the sons of God. Thus will it be that we too will be given the choice to serve or not to serve!

- The same woman Jesus addressed at His first public miracle by the word "woman."
- The same woman Jesus addressed from the cross as "woman."
- The same woman who is preparing the three measures of meal—the Bread of Life Everlasting—the Marriage Supper of the Lamb—Heaven's Wedding Feast.

The woman, of course, is the Immaculate Virgin Mary. And so if the Virgin Mary, the Blessed Mother, gave birth to Jesus' First Coming, it shouldn't be so difficult to believe that through her apparitions that are increasing throughout the world she is giving birth to His Second Coming—the unveiling/revelation of the sons of God. Note that the woman, who is *full of grace,*[110] never calls attention to herself. She always points to her Son and says *Do as He tells you.* Her messages echo her Son's: pray, fast and do penance—the Kingdom of God is at hand.

THE MARRIAGE SUPPER OF THE LAMB

Traditionally the woman of the house prepared the meals for her spouse and their children. As did the Virgin Mary prepare the meals for Jesus and His foster father Joseph, Mary's spouse in the natural order. Therefore, as we take into account that God uses the natural to reveal the supernatural, it would correspond that God's spouse in the supernatural order, the Immaculate Virgin Mary, would be preparing the meal for Him as well as all His children.

---

110 *And the angel being come in, said unto her: Hail, full of grace, the Lord is with thee: blessed art thou among women* (St. Luke 1:29).

Thus it shouldn't be surprising that "the meal" she is preparing is Heaven's Wedding Feast—*the Marriage Supper of the Lamb* [111]— the Bread of Everlasting Life. Her recipe is simple: She is using three measures of water, salt, and virgin olive oil to unite the finest wheat flour into bread dough—the meal. This is the very meal Jesus is referring to in Matthew 13:33 when He says, *"The Kingdom of heaven is like to leaven, which 'a woman' took and hid in three measures of meal, until the whole was leavened."*

The Conception of Jesus—the Bread of Eternal Life: In the natural order, conception of a human being takes place when a man and a woman become one flesh and the male's sperm, through the miraculous grace of God, unites with the female's egg.

This reflects what took place in the supernatural order when Jesus was conceived, in that at Jesus' conception the Cloud of God's Glory (the water and salt from Heaven's Sea) that overshadowed Mary can be likened to the male sperm; whereas the Virgin Mary's virgin olive oil (oil from paradise/earth) can be likened to the female egg.

All the other elements in Jesus' Body and Blood were from His Mother's human nature and of the earth. These are the elements of this world St. Paul is referring to in Colossians 2:20 when he says *"If then you be dead with Christ from the elements of this world..."* We, like Jesus, must overcome these elements which keep us weighted down.

The Sacred Unity of the Holy Spirit with His beloved Spouse: At the most elevated part of the Mass—the Great Doxology—the Priest proclaims: "Through Him, and with Him, and in Him, O

---

111 Revelation 19:9:*And he said to me: Write: Blessed are they that are called to <u>the marriage supper of the Lamb.</u> And he saith to me: These words of God are true.*

God, almighty Father, <u>in the Unity of the Holy Spirit</u> – all glory and honor is yours, forever and ever. Amen."

This Unity epitomizes the Holy Spirit's Sacred Act of Divine Oneness with His beloved and Immaculate Spouse the Virgin Mary. It is within this very Sacred Act of Unity that Mary conceived Jesus— the Father's only begotten Son. And it is through this very Sacred Act of Unity repeated at every Holy Sacrifice of the Mass that we enter mystically into Sacred Unity—Holy Communion—with them.

It is because of this most Sacred Act of Unity we are able to proclaim that Jesus, the God-Man, is the glorious manifestation of God's love for His beloved Spouse.

It is through the perpetual love of God that dwells in this Most Holy and Most Sacred Act of Unity that God is drawing and sanctifying all things in Heaven and on earth to Himself.

112

---

112 Murillo, Esteban Bartoleme "The Annunciation."

THE UNITY OF THE HOLY SPIRIT

The knowledge of God's love for His beloved Spouse and their act of Sacred Unity that conceived their Son's consubstantial—Divine and Human—nature, is the focal point of the Gospel of the Holy Spirit that will be preached to all the nations.

The Gospel of the Holy Spirit entails the revelation that Jesus Christ's risen and glorified Flesh is comprised of His Father's Life Giving Water and Sanctifying Salt—as well as His Immaculate Virgin Mother's purest and most holy Virgin Olive Oil!

Through these three sacred elements, dispensed to us in the seven sacraments, we enter into their Sacred Unity—the Unity of the Holy Spirit. *"For both He that sanctifieth, and they who are sanctified, are all one."* (Hebrews 2:11)

The Testimony of Jesus Christ: The knowledge and understanding in this unveiling of the substance of Jesus' risen Flesh of Glory and how we come to partake of it, is the testimony of Jesus Christ that the Two Olive Trees (*the sons of oil*—the sons of Mary) are to give witness to: *"And when they shall have finished 'their testimony,' the beast [the anti-Christ—the anti-anointed one]...shall overcome them and kill them (Rev. 11:7). And after three days and a half the spirit of life from God entered them. And they went up to heaven in a cloud: and their enemies saw them."* (Rev. 11:11&12)

As we proceed into the next chapter of Revelation, the one in which the Woman of the Unveiling is further described, we read: *"And the dragon was angry against 'the woman': and went to make war with her seed, who keep the commandments of God, and have 'the testimony of Jesus Christ."* (Rev. 12:17) Recall that the dragon, the serpent

Lucifer, hates the Woman because God chose Her above him to conceive and give birth to His Son.

The Woman's children are the seed who accept the testimony of Jesus Christ now being unveiled. The testimony reveals the mystery of the full knowledge of Our Lord and Savior Jesus Christ's risen and glorified Flesh dispensed to us through the seven sacraments and "now" rising up into fullness within us.

St. Paul is referring to this hidden mystery when he writes, ***But we speak 'the wisdom of God' in 'a mystery', a wisdom which is 'hidden,' which God ordained before the world, unto our Glory.***" (1 Cor. 2:7) The mystery and wisdom of God's Glory hidden within us and how we come to share in "It"[113] is now being revealed.

This is the testimony of Jesus that the souls of this last time will be beheaded for: "*...and the souls of them that were beheaded for the testimony of Jesus, and for the Word of God, and who had not adored the beast nor his image, nor received his character[114] on their foreheads, or in their hands; and they lived and reigned with Christ a thousand years.*" (Revelations 20:4)

St. Paul was beheaded for his testimony of Jesus. In the same way, in this last time, many of us will also be beheaded for the testimony of Jesus now being revealed.

The preaching of this wondrous knowledge on the Sacred Substance and Sacred Unity of the Holy Spirit and the fullness that dwells therein, explains why Jesus said: "*Whosoever shall say a word*

---

113 "It" is one of the few words italicized in the Douay-Rheims Bible, as seen in John 16:14-15 "*He shall glorify me; because He shall receive of mine, and shall show 'It' to you. All things whatsoever the Father hath are mine. Therefore I said, that he shall receive of mine and show 'It' to you.*

114 The character on their foreheads, or in their hands, is the mark of the beast. The mark of the beast will likely be a microchip implanted in the forehead or hand without which no one will be able to buy or sell. Those who refuse to accept this microchip will live and reign with Christ Jesus during the new era of peace as seen in Revelation 20:4. For those who accept the mark – there is no salvation – as seen in Revelation 14:9-11. See also Revelation 13:16-18.

against the Son of man, it shall be forgiven him; but he that shall speak against the Holy Ghost, it shall not be forgiven him, neither in this world, nor in the world to come. Either make the <u>tree good</u> and its <u>fruit good</u>; or make <u>the tree evil</u>, and its <u>fruit evil</u>. For by the fruit the tree is known." (Matthew 12:32-33)

Note how Jesus in speaking out about the sin against the Holy Ghost compares this fatal sin to speaking against a good tree and its good fruit—the tree and fruit being a metaphor for parents and child. This mystical metaphor is used to make the point that the fruit—as in child, is of the same substance of the tree—the child's parents. Therefore, this parable is meant to convey that Jesus—the good fruit, is inseparable from both His Father and Mother—the Good Tree. (In the same way the evil fruit—the antichrist, is inseparable from the evil tree—Lucifer.)

Therefore, the fatal sin against the Holy Spirit is the fatal sin against Jesus' parents, but in a more particular way against "the Woman" who gave birth to His Human Nature—His Immaculate Mother, the Virgin Mary, who in Scripture, as we shall now see, is referred to as both "the Tree of Life" and "the Good Tree."

The Good Tree, Lady Wisdom, is a Tree of Life: The Book of Proverbs Chapter 3 provides abundant insight into the knowledge of the good tree and its good fruit. This chapter discourses on Lady Wisdom, the beautiful and peaceable Spouse of God, who in this Book is referred to as "a tree of life." The following excerpts are taken from verses 13-19: *"Blessed is the man that findeth **wisdom**; The purchasing thereof is better than the merchandise of silver, and **her fruit** than the chiefest and <u>purest gold</u>; She is more precious than all riches; Her ways are beautiful ways and all her paths are peaceable; **She is a tree of life** to those that lay hold of her; and he that shall retain her is blessed."*

Note how Lady Wisdom is referred to as *"a tree of life"* (indicative of the good tree in Jesus' parable) whose *"fruit"* (indicative of the good fruit in Jesus' parable) is more precious than the finest gold. Of course the only fruit more precious than the finest gold is Jesus. Thus, the Tree of Life that produced this fruit—Lady Wisdom—is

---

115 A copyright could not be found on this beautiful depiction of Our Lady of the Revelation (whose mantle is of the color "olive green") with the Holy Trinity. Note the "3" SEAshells at the bottom!

none other than Jesus' blessed Mother, the Immaculate Virgin Mary!

The Evil Tree, Lucifer, is The Tree of Death: The evil tree in the above parable is Lucifer and his spouse, the harlot of Babylon, who together produces the evil fruit—the **"anti-Christ!"** The anti-Christ, whose name means **"against the Anointed One."**

Wisdom pay attention: Why is the anti-Christ so vehemently against "the Anointed One?" Because the Anointed One's anointing—with the purest and finest virgin golden olive oil, comes from the "Olive Tree" whom God favored above him. She is "the Good Tree of Life." Lucifer, the anti-Christ, is the "evil tree of death."

Christ – the Anointed: The name Jesus means "Savior," the name Christ means "Anointed One." Jesus' humanity was clothed with the flesh flowing from the blood of His Immaculate Virgin Mother Mary. Her blood, which at Jesus' conception united with the Father's Sea of Glory, contained the elements of this world that Jesus would overcome—as well as the purest golden Virgin Olive Oil that anointed and sealed His precious Body and Blood in the Sacred Love and Unity of the Holy Spirit.

The Sin against Lady Wisdom in who dwells the Gifts of the Holy Spirit: For further insight into the sin against the Holy Spirit for which there is no forgiveness, let's go back to Proverbs 8:3 where Lady Wisdom is speaking about her fruit that is better than gold and precious stone. In this verse Lady Wisdom is *"standing in the top of the highest places by the way, in the midst of the paths, besides the gates of the city, in the very doors she speaketh"* beckoning the little and unwise ones to receive her instruction.

From this position, beside the gates of the New Jerusalem, Lady Wisdom proceeds to teach about *"the great things and the right things"* inherent to Her: wisdom, knowledge, understanding, fear of the

Lord, counsel, courage, and piety. These great and righteous things are gifts of the Holy Spirit! For example, in Proverbs 8:12 Lady Wisdom says, *"I wisdom dwell in counsel, and am present in learned thoughts."*

Now does this imply that Lady Wisdom is the Holy Spirit? Not at all, however it does mean that God and His Spouse are one in unity—Sacred Unity. What is His is also Hers. After all, in the words of the Archangel Gabriel, She is "full of grace!!!"

This enlightening chapter of Proverbs climatically ends: *"He that shall find me, shall find 'life', and shall have salvation from the Lord: but he that shall sin against me, shall hurt his own soul. All that hate me love 'death.''* (Proverbs 8:36)

In other words, he that finds "the woman" Lady Wisdom finds the Good Tree of Life—the Immaculate Virgin Mary, the Spouse of the Holy Spirit; and, He that hates her loves the evil tree of death—Lucifer!

Noting, once again, how this prophetic verse links the sin of speaking out against the Holy Spirit with the sin against Lady Wisdom, both sharing the same horrible demise—death of the soul.

Apparently God in His Divine meekness will let you speak out against His Son's humanity, which was crucified to the cross. However, if you dare to speak out against His Sacred Unity with His beloved inviolate Spouse, who bore the fruit of His risen Flesh of Glory, Jesus, then, like any valiant man of honor He will come to her defense and you will suffer grave and eternal consequences: *"Either make the fruit good and its tree good or make the fruit evil and its tree evil!"*

The Blasphemies against the Holy Spirit and Lady Wisdom are seen in Revelations 13:6. These blasphemies of the beast are: against God's Name (the Holy Spirit); against His Tabernacle (Mary); and against them that dwell in Heaven (the Saints).

In the New Covenant Jesus tells us that the blasphemy against the Holy Spirit is the sin for which there is no forgiveness. He summarizes this with the parable: *"Either make the tree good and its fruit good; or make the tree evil and its fruit evil."* This shows that the blasphemy is against the Sacred Unity of the Father and the Mother (the Good Tree) whose love produces Jesus (the Good fruit).

In the Old Covenant we saw it written that he who finds Wisdom finds the Tree of Life (the Good Tree of the Olive, the Immaculate Virgin Mother of God), and he who sins or blasphemes against her, "hurts his own soul, loves death, the tree of death, the evil tree. Again, this suggests that the blasphemy is against the Immaculate Virgin Mother of God.

The blasphemies against God: Now as we go to the Book of Revelations Chapter 13 we see the culmination of evil taking place in the blasphemies of the beast against God. More specifically the blasphemies are against: God's Name, God's Tabernacle, and them that dwell in Heaven: *"And he [the beast] opened his mouth unto blasphemies against God, to blaspheme His Name [the Holy Spirit], and His tabernacle [His Immaculate Virgin Mother Mary], and them that dwell in heaven [the saints]."* (Rev. 13:6)

"Come Eat my Bread and Drink the Wine which I have Mingled for you": Then as we go from Chapter 8 of Proverbs, which depicts Lady Wisdom, to Chapter 9 we learn that Lady Wisdom is inviting all to the Feast she has prepared (the three measures of meal—the Marriage Supper of the Lamb). Listen attentively: *"Wisdom hath built us a house [the Body of Christ - the Church[116]"]; she hath hewn her out seven pillars [the seven sacraments]. She hath slain her victims [Her beloved Jesus and beloved priest Sons] mingled her wine [their Blood], and*

---

116 Mary's Virgin olive oil is what gives "structure" to Jesus' resurrected Body of Glory and since her virgin olive oil provides the structure of God's Mystical Body, the Church, this is likely one reason the Church has come to be known as the Bride of Christ.

set forth her table. She hath sent her maids [5 virgins carrying their lamps filled with the purest and chiefest Virgin Olive Oil] to invite to the tower, and to the walls of the city [the New Jerusalem]. Whosoever is a little one [childlike, humble and lowly] let him come to me. And to the unwise [those who have not entered into the fullness of the One, Holy, Catholic, and Apostolic Church] she said: **'Come, eat my Bread, and drink the wine which I have mingled for you."** (Proverbs 9:1-5)

What an awesome invitation to enter into the Paschal Mystery— the Wedding Supper of the Lamb (the New Passover), the celebration of the holy sacrifice of the Mass, where the risen Bread of Life Everlasting (the three measures of meal prepared in the Woman's oven—the womb of the Immaculate Virgin Mary) is being served.

Please ponder: When Jesus at the Last Supper held up the Bread saying, "This is my Body" and held up the wine saying, "This is my Blood," was not His Body and Blood which was united in oneness with His Father and Holy Spirit, also mystically united in oneness with His Mother who clothed His Flesh and Blood in the purest and most precious fruit of the olive?

The Olive Tree made known: In the parable about the tree and its fruit Jesus makes an important point of saying: *"By the fruit the tree is known."* Jesus, the fruit, spoke these words because He wants to make known the tree — His Mother the Olive Tree. She is the Good Tree of Life — to whom the two olive trees — *"the sons of oil"* are to give witness.

Jesus wants to make it known that His Blessed Mother is "the Woman" who clothed His Divine and Human nature in the purest of golden fruit—the Immaculate Virgin Olive. God has elevated Mary above all and wants us to come to recognize her worthiness, and to come to know and love her as He does.

So if you think about it, those who dare to speak out against the Immaculate Virgin Mary when the Gospel of the Holy Spirit is proclaimed, these, as Lady Wisdom forewarned, sin against her and hurt their souls, they love death. <u>Remember that Lucifer was jealous of the Woman and hated her from the beginning!</u>

Jesus also wants to make known the evil tree and the evil fruit—the serpent Lucifer and his cohorts. In this last time these evil ones will try to coerce man to blaspheme:

* The Holy Spirit: The Sacred Name of God's Divine Oneness in love, substance and unity. The blessed and holy Name through which Our Father's Name is hallowed—crowned with Glory—given all the praise, love, thanksgiving and honor it is so deserving of!
* The Queen Mother: The Good Olive Tree who is the Tree of Life, Lady Wisdom, the Blessed Virgin Mary and the Mother of God!
* The Saints who accept and embrace this manifestation of Truth—the Gospel of the Holy Spirit – the Gospel of Christ's Glory.

<u>The Seeds of the Good Fruit made known</u>: These seeds love truth and life, they are prolife! They grow in the light of Wisdom and manifest as the following fruits of the Holy Spirit: kindness, gentleness, goodness, generosity, self sacrifice/longsuffering, love of God and neighbor, chastity, joy, faithfulness, peace, modesty—everything beautiful, peaceable, and good.

<u>The Seeds of the Evil fruit made known</u>: These seeds love death and lies. They grow in the darkness of hatred and manifest in pride, jealously, lust, envy, self indulgence, idolatry, murder—everything

ugly, confusing, and evil. They are against God's law and natural order.

The First and Last Books of the Bible: It's notable that the parable Jesus uses to give insight into the fatal sin against the Holy Spirit takes us back to the Book of Genesis, where it is in the Garden of Eden that both the *"Tree of Life"* and the *"Tree of the Knowledge of Good and Evil,"* dwell in the midst of all the other trees that are pleasant to eat (Genesis 2:9).

In this first book of the Bible God is speaking of the "seeds of life" (the saints) who come through the "Tree of Life" (the Woman), and the "seeds of death," (the souls of the damned) who come from the "tree of death" (Lucifer), when He says to the serpent in the Garden of Eden: *"I will put enmities between thee and the woman, and thy seed and her seed; she shall crush thy head and thou shalt lie in wait for her heel."* Recalling, once again, the enmity that existed between Lucifer and the "the Woman" from the beginning (Genesis 3:15).

Then as we go to the last Book of the Bible—the Book of Revelation, we are reminded of the enmity between the serpent and the Woman and her seed: *"And the dragon [the serpent/devil/ Satan/Lucifer] <u>was angry with the woman</u> [The Blessed Mother of God/ the Immaculate Virgin Mary], and went to make war with the rest of her seed [the saints], who keep the commandments of God, <u>and have the testimony of Jesus Christ."</u>* (Revelations 12:17)

The testimony of Jesus Christ is the full knowledge of Christ's risen substance of Glory that is now being declared. The testimony entails how Jesus Christ's risen substance of Glory is comprised of the elements of water, salt and olive oil. These elements, the first elements, are *those things* that are administered to us through the seven sacraments of the Church. This knowledge of the substance of Christ's risen Glory is the Gospel of the Holy Ghost that must be "preached again" in order to bring about our sanctification. Of this Gospel, St. Peter writes:

> *"Searching what or what manner of time the Spirit of Christ in them did signify: when it foretold those sufferings that are in Christ, and the 'glories that should follow': To whom it was revealed, that not to themselves, 'but to you' they ministered 'those things' [water, salt, and oil – substance/unity] which are 'now declared[117]' to you by them that have PREACHED THE GOSPEL TO YOU, THE HOLY GHOST being sent down from heaven on whom the angels desire to look. Wherefore having the loins of your mind girt up, being sober, TRUST PERFECTLY IN THE GRACE WHICH IS OFFERED YOU IN THE REVELATION OF JESUS CHRIST, as children of obedience, not fashioned according to the former desires of your ignorance."*
> (I Peter vs. 11-14)

You must know that most of Lucifer's energy, and hatred has a lot of energy, is aimed at deceitfully and cunningly[118] diminishing the Woman's role in God's plan of salvation as well as in attacking her seed—the One Holy Catholic and Apostolic Church.

The things that shall be have already been: and God restoreth that which is past **(Ecclesiastes 3:15):** When the Two Olive Trees give witness to this testimony of the revelation of Jesus Christ, the Gospel of the Holy Ghost, those of the seed of the Woman

---

117 Recall in the Book of Isaiah how the Lord promised that before "the new things spring forth" he would "declare them?" He is NOW, in what St. Paul refers to as DUE TIME, declaring them.

118 Lucifer hides behind good works: *For such false apostles are deceitful workmen, transforming themselves into the apostles of Christ. And no wonder: for Satan himself transformeth himself into an angel of light* (2 Corinthians 11:13-14). Pray to discern the infiltrators in the Church, the wolves in sheep's clothing, who are the false apostles hiding behind good works.

will embrace this manifestation of the Gospel of Truth with love and devotion. Whereas those of the seed of the serpent Satan will blaspheme it, and this, once again, is the sin for which there is no forgiveness!

In this last time Lucifer and his cohorts' fury will rage more violently than ever before on earth. This battle will culminate on Mt. Zion where Jesus' Mystical Head—the 144,000 virgin Marian Priests, in whose mouth is found no lie because they will have preached this eternal Gospel of Truth, go to the cross. The Good News is that they rise again glorious to live in the love, peace, substance and sacred unity of the Holy Ghost."

The martyrdom of these "little sacrificial lambs" of God brings about the renewal of all of Christianity.

The Christians who follow in their footsteps are led to the great beheading—as revealed in the Book of Revelation chapter 20:4. These all rise from the dead, and live and reign with Christ—God's anointed and beloved Marian Priest Sons—for the 1000 year period of Peace, the Church's honeymoon, the New Spring-time.

The Choice of Life or Death: In Deuteronomy 30:19 God sets before us, as He did the angels, the tree of life and the tree of death: *"I call heaven and earth to witness this day, that I have set before you Life [the Woman] and death [the serpent Lucifer], blessing and cursing, choose therefore Life [the Good Tree of life], that both thou and thy seed may live."*

You must choose to accept and serve the great sign of Revelation 12—the Woman clothed with the sun... being with child... laboring in pain... the child SOON to be delivered.

A great and grave battle rages for our souls. Lucifer and his evil cohorts have already made their choice. These angels who love death, now prowl the world seeking to devour souls. It is time to pray, fast, and do penance for ourselves and our loved ones because the kingdom of darkness—the kingdom of yeast, is rising up against the Kingdom of Light—the salt of the earth.

Lucifer, the false light bearer, has hated "the Woman"—whose heel is to crush his head, from the beginning. You must therefore choose to love and honor her for she is the Good Olive Tree of Life to whom the Two Olive Trees, the sons of Oil, will bear witness to every nation, people, kingdom, and tongue.

In the very last chapter of the Bible, Revelations 22:14, St. John the beloved writes: *"Blessed are they that wash their robes in the Blood of the Lamb: that they may have a right to the Tree of Life, and may enter in by the gates into the city."* This takes us back to Proverbs 8:3, where Wisdom (the Spouse of the Holy Spirit, the Mother of Jesus) is standing beside the gates of the city, the New Jerusalem, from where she is presently instructing the unwise and inviting the little ones to the Feast she has prepared—the three measures of Meal, the Marriage Supper of the Lamb—*"Come eat my Bread, and drink the Wine I have prepared for you."*

CHAPTER 11

§

"Let us be glad and rejoice,
and give 'Glory' to Him;
for the Marriage of the Lamb is come,
and His bride hath prepared herself.
And it is granted to her that she should clothe herself
with fine linen, glittering and white.
For the fine linen are the justifications of the saints."

REVELATIONS 19:7-8

The Marriage Covenant is bound through: An Outer Unveiling, An Inner Unveiling, A New Name

§

THE FOLLOWING SHOWS HOW THE marriage covenant between a bride and groom in the natural realm corresponds to the marriage of Christ—the Groom, to His Bride—the Church, in the supernatural realm.

1.) **The Outer Unveiling:** The white veil, representing purity, is worn by the bride over her head and face to conceal her radiant beauty. The marriage ceremony begins with the bride, who is both dressed and veiled in white, walking down the aisle escorted by her father. It isn't until she approaches the sanctuary that the outer white veil is lifted and her groom, whom she now meets face to face, is able to behold her beauty. Solemn vows are then spoken, exchanged, and sealed with a holy kiss.

This corresponds to the Mystery of Christ's Marriage to His Church because Christ's Bride is also veiled in white and escorted by the Father. This is first seen in the Old Testament where the white veil is represented by the Cloud of God's Glory—the Cloud through which the Father escorted His people into the Promise Land.

It is next seen in the New Testament where the veil is represented by the seven sacraments which veil the Bride's brilliant white beauty—too bright for our eyes yet to behold. The sacraments come to us through God the Father who gave us His only begotten Son, Jesus, through whose Blood our wedding garments are washed and made "white" as seen in Revelations 7:14: *"These are they who are come out of the great tribulation, and have washed their robes, and have made them 'white' in the blood of the Lamb."* (Recall that when the seven colors of the rainbow, analogous to the seven sacraments, are reversed through a triangular prism, analogous to the Holy Trinity, they come out white.)

To know God is to love God, therefore when the full knowledge of God's Glory is loved, honored, cherished and openly proclaimed by the Church—His Bride, the veil will be lifted and we shall behold Him face to face. Our solemn vows will also be sealed with a holy kiss—the holy kiss of Peace.

2.) **The Inner Unveiling:** After the marriage ceremony and the feasting with family and friends, the bride and groom enter into their private chamber where the inner unveiling takes place. The renting of the hymen by the risen circumcised dome represents the inner unveiling. Once this veil is rent, blood flows forth and entry is made into the inner womb, the sacred sanctuary, of the bride where the unity of oneness takes place. The climactic outpouring that ensues consummates the marriage. The womb now open is able to conceive new life.

This is analogous to Christ's marriage to His Bride, the Church, because it too is bound together in virgin blood: First in the virgin Blood of Jesus flowing from His Sacred Heart rent— unveiled—on the cross. Next, in the virgin blood of the martyrs who for the last two thousand years have followed in His footsteps; and finally, in the virgin blood of the Marian Priests—the 144,000 celibate virgins whose blood shedding is to take place on Mount Zion as foretold in the Book of Revelation 14:1-6. *"These follow the Lamb[119] whithersoever he goeth."* (Rev. 14:4)

This copious shedding of blood,[120] which corresponds to the renting/unveiling of the Bride's hymen, comes when the Church proclaims the Gospel of the Holy Spirit (I Peter 1:12) and with heartfelt love and affection invokes the ejaculation **"Come Holy Spirit, come, by means of the powerful intercession of the Immaculate Heart of Mary thy well beloved Spouse."**[121] The climactic outpouring of God's Glory—the Great Consummation—ensues. The sacred womb now open, conceives and springs-forth new life—our new and glorified life in the New Jerusalem.

---

119 In Revelations chapter 14:1 we see where *the lamb* who is standing on Mount Sion with the 144,000, is a "little lamb or lambkin." We know this because the word lamb here is not capitalized – the diminutive is used to convey a slighter degree of its root meaning. Whereas in Rev. 14:4 *the Lamb* is capitalized, thus referring to Jesus the Lamb of God! This was pointed out to me by Father Joachim using the Douay Rheims Bible – a strict Word for Word translation of the Latin Vulgate. The little lamb would therefore be a chosen son of God, most likely a Pope, who leads his faithful and true 144,000 virgin Marian priests, in complete and perfect oneness with Jesus, on the road to Calvary.

120 In Blessed Anne Catherine Emmerick's <u>The Revelation of the Life of Christ</u>, she writes: "I saw Noah offering sacrifice in the ark upon an altar covered with a red cloth over which was a white cloth." Vol. 1, pg. 39; Then on page 227, "And now the Blessed Virgin swathed the Child in red and over that in a white veil…" These are two of the numerous times a white cloth—representing God's Glory, covers a red cloth—representing His Blood.

121 This beautiful ejaculation was given to Father Gobbi of the Marian Movement of Priests by Our Lady.

A depth of insight into this powerful ejaculation, which brings about the coming of the Holy Spirit, is realized in the following teaching of Judaism: "There are two terms for the sexual act. The better known term is that which is used in the Bible and Talmud, bi'ah, which means 'a coming' as in 'he came unto her.' The second term, also quite relevant, is "a Kabbalistic term, chibbur, which means 'joining.' It is used in 'The Book of Joining of Man and His Wife." [122]

We must keep in mind that our Heavenly Father's mystical Kingdom is a reflection of the Gospel of Un-circumcision given to St. Paul to preach. This is a spiritual Kingdom which springs forth from the circumcision of our hearts—not the flesh! However, it was mystically manifested in the flesh, when Jesus' Heart, on the cross, was pierced by the lance and Blood and Water flowed forth. The heart itself, with its four chambers and double dome formation contains many mysteries which reflect the Old and New Covenant.

After the Great Consummation, which coincides with the inner unveiling, the earth quakes and the dead rise from their tombs to live and reign with "Christ" —"God's anointed Priest sons." Recall that an earthquake and rising from the dead also took place after Jesus' martyrdom, once again calling to mind the Scripture: *the things that shall be, have already been: and God restoreth that which is past [paradise].*" (Ecclesiastes 3:15) Paradise is restored when everything comes full circle.

This reign of Christ is the thousand year period of peace foretold in Revelation 20:4. This glorious day in the Lord corresponds to the Bride's, the Church's honeymoon. It is

---

122 From the textbook The Art of Marriage pg. 49, published by the Rohr Jewish Learning Institute.

a New Era of love, of holiness and of peace! Our Lady often speaks of this New Era in her book "<u>To the Priests, Our Lady's Beloved Sons</u>[123]"

(The climactic culmination involving the martyrdom of the last time saints, is well depicted in the text of the Third Secret of Fatima: "And we [the visionaries] saw in an immense light that is God: something similar to how people appear in a mirror when they pass in front of it, a Bishop [little lamb] dressed in White we had the impression that it was the Holy Father. Other Bishops, Priests, men and women religious going up a steep mountain, at the top of which there was a big Cross of rough-hewn trunks as of a cork tree with the bark; before reaching there the Holy Father passed through a big city half in ruins and half trembling with halting step, afflicted with pain and sorrow, he prayed for the souls of the corpses he met on his way; having reached the top of the mountain, on his knees at the foot of the big Cross he was killed by a group of soldiers who fired bullets and arrows at him, and in the same way there died one after another the other Bishops, Priests, men and women Religious, and various lay people of different ranks and positions. Beneath the two arms of the Cross there were two Angels each with a crystal aspersorium in his hand, in which they gathered up the blood of the Martyrs and with it sprinkled the souls that were making their way to God." As you may know, St. John Paul II believed that the fulfillment of this prophecy took place when he was shot on Our Lady of Fatima's feast day of May 13, 1981, however there are mystics and theologians who don't agree.)

---

123 To the Priests, Our Lady's Beloved Sons: 392j; 231i; 236e; 324h; 336f; 549j; 366f; and, 388l.

3.) **A New Name:** Traditionally the family name expressed the family's essence and identity. Thus, with the bride's willingness to change her name to a new name she was saying yes to becoming one with her husband's essence; yes, to taking on his identity; yes, to bringing his desires to fulfillment; and yes, to submitting to his authority and will, until death do them part.

In the same way, a new name corresponds to Christ's Marriage to His Bride, the Church, as seen in Revelations 3:12: *"He that shall overcome [the crucifixion of the Marian Priests and the beheadings which follow] I will make him a pillar in the temple of my God; and he shall go out no more; and I will write upon him the Name of My God, and <u>the name of the city of my God, the New Jerusalem</u>, which cometh down out of heaven from my God, and <u>my New Name</u>."*

Of this day of great joy and prosperity in the Church Zacharias 14:9 states: *"And the Lord shall be king over all the earth; in that day there shall be <u>one Lord, and His Name shall be one</u>!"* [124]

The New Jerusalem, as seen in Revelation 3:12, is traditionally understood by the Church to be Mary. She and Her Spouse share the New Name, the Holy Spirit, which expresses their Divine Oneness, because through marriage they have become "one flesh." St. Paul in Ephesians 5:31-32 is speaking of Marriage, which he calls a *"great sacrament."* when he writes *"they shall be two in 'one flesh."*

This marvelous mystery is confirmed in the book 33 Days of Morning Glory, by the author, Father Michael E. Gaitley, MIC, who quotes St. Maximillian Kolbe as saying: "If among

---

124 In verse 4 of this same chapter of Zachariah, the Word of God refers to the Mount of Olives and, in verse 8 to the sea!

human beings the wife takes the name of her husband because she belongs to him, is one with him, becomes equal to him and is, with him, the source of new life, **with how much greater reason should the name of the Holy Spirit, who is the divine Immaculate Conception, be used as the name of her in whom he lives as uncreated Love,** the principle of life in the whole supernatural order of grace." (pg. 54, bold added)

Therefore, in the supernatural order of grace, the Immaculate Virgin Mary has taken on a New Name, that of her beloved Spouse, the Holy Spirit! The Holy Spirit sanctifies and glorifies the New Jerusalem, His beloved Spouse.

We are now able to grasp the understanding of the Sacred Unity and Divine Oneness that the Holy Spirit has with His Beloved Virgin Spouse!

What's even more amazing is that God's people, through the Church, are able to enter into this same sacred Marriage Covenant through their worthy reception of the seven sacraments, which dispenses the sacred substance of God's Divine Oneness to us: water, salt and virgin olive oil. Thus, we too shall come to share in the New Name commencing with our Baptism: In the Name of the Holy Spirit!

<u>The Holy Ghost being sent down from Heaven on whom the angels desire to look:</u> It is also quite fascinating to ponder how the Third Person of the Holy Trinity is invisible from all eternity, that is, until through the Holy Spirit's marriage, which took place in time and space, to the Immaculate Virgin Mary, He has taken on a new dimension: the purest of virgin olive oil which can be looked upon!

This wonderful knowledge of God which expresses His Sacred Unity and Divine Oneness with His beloved Spouse, and also His

Church, is the Gospel of the Holy Ghost[125] that St. Peter, repeating once again, is referring to in the following: *"Searching what or what manner of time the Spirit of Christ in them did signify: when it foretold those sufferings that are in Christ, and the 'glories that should follow': To whom it was revealed, that not to themselves, but to you they ministered 'those things' [water, salt, and oil – the substance of God's Glory] which are now declared to you by them that have PREACHED THE GOSPEL TO YOU, THE HOLY GHOST being sent down from heaven on whom the angels desire to look [the angels are able to look, as in see, because the Gospel of the Holy Ghost is the knowledge of the risen and glorified Flesh of Jesus, whose substance has visibility]. Wherefore having the loins of your mind girt up, being sober, TRUST PERFECTLY IN THE GRACE WHICH IS OFFERED YOU IN THE REVELATION OF JESUS CHRIST, as children of obedience, not fashioned according to the former desires of your ignorance."* (1Peter 1:11-13)

In a nutshell, The Gospel of the Holy Ghost is the knowledge of God's Love for His beloved spouse as well as the knowledge of the substance of their Sacred Unity and Divine Oneness which conceived their Son Jesus—God's Divine and Human Nature.

The Gospel of the Holy Ghost also reveals how we enter into their Sacred Unity and Divine Oneness through Jesus' humanity—glorified in His death and resurrection—in our worthy reception of the seven sacraments. The grace offered us in this Revelation of Jesus Christ is the knowledge that Christ's substance of Glory is comprised of both His Heavenly Father's Sea and His Immaculate Mother's Virgin Olive Oil!

---

125 Because this new dimension of the Holy Spirit has visibility, this is likely where the origin in the distinction of the Holy Spirit and the Holy Ghost in the old time Bible came about, in that a spirit has no visibility whereas a ghost, the visibility of a dead person, can be seen, looked upon! Hence, the manifestation of the substance of Jesus' risen dead body was seen as the manifestation of a ghost!

The revelation of the full knowledge of the Son of God now being made known is so eloquently expressed in this most edifying teaching of Judaism, Rashi, Genesis 2:24, on the "fruit" of Marriage: **"The Child is formed by them both, and—in the child— they become one flesh."**[126]

In other words, in the child Jesus—both God the Holy Spirit and His beloved Spouse, the Immaculate Virgin Mary, have become "ONE FLESH! (Whose Flesh on whom the angels desire to look.)

It is Jesus' risen and glorified Flesh that reveals the Holy Spirit "fully" because His Glorified Flesh is the sanctifying substance through, with and in which "all things" in Heaven and earth are uniting into sacred oneness and rising into fullness. Recollecting the Catechism's teaching, "Jesus did not reveal the Holy Spirit 'fully' until His death and resurrection when He has been glorified, but little by little He alluded to Him as when He said 'His own Flesh [The risen elements of His Body – the substance of His Glory] will be food for the life of the world (CCC section 728, underlined added).

This knowledge of Jesus' risen and glorified Body/Flesh is necessary *"For the perfecting of the saints, for the work of the ministry, for the edifying of the body of Christ; Until we all meet into the unity of faith, and of the knowledge of the Son of God, unto a perfect man, unto 'the measure" of the age of the 'fullness' of Christ."* (Ephesians 4:12-13)

The measure of the age of the fullness of Christ brings to mind the parable of the three measures of meal (the Kingdom of Heaven) that is rising into fullness. Recall the Woman is using three measures of water, salt and olive oil to unite her meal.

Back to the Marriage Covenant: We enter into the marriage covenant with Jesus when we lovingly say yes, FIAT, to entering into divine oneness with His Bride, the Church. Our Covenant

---

126 From the textbook The Art of Marriage, pg. 39, published by the Rohr Jewish Learning Institute.

Marriage with Jesus takes place through the seven sacraments: In the Name of the Father, in the Name of the Son, and in the Name of the Holy Spirit.

It is through our love, reverence and faithfulness to all seven of the sacraments, His Mystical Body, that we are bringing our Bridegroom's desires into perfection and completion. And, it is through our obedience to the Church's Magisterium that we come to submit to God's Holy and Divine Will until death, bringing about our glorified new life—in the love, peace, joy and unity of the Holy Spirit! [127]

The Book of Apocalypse, also known as the Book of Revelation: As God would have it, the unveiling of Jesus Christ within us coincides with the unveiling of the apocalyptical events John gives us an account of in the Book of Revelation—the Book of the Unveiling! For this reason the Book of the Revelation begins: *"The Revelation [Unveiling] of Jesus Christ, which God gave unto him, to make known to his servants the things which must shortly come to pass..."* St. John, like St. Paul, was shown the future events which have now started to unfold before our eyes.

It is no coincidence that in Jesus' time the word "apocalypse" referred to the "unveiling" that took place when two virgins, after feasting with family and friends for seven days, entered into the

---

127 God uses the natural to reveal His supernatural plan of salvation: In order for a man to have legitimate heirs he needs to be married. This is because it is through his bride that the children of his flesh and blood are conceived and brought forth into life. It is no different for our Bridegroom, Jesus, through whose Bride, the Church, His legitimate heirs are conceived. Our conception takes place through His Flesh and Blood shed on the Cross and dispensed to us in the 7 sacraments, most powerfully in Holy Communion/the Bread of Life. Pay heed to these words from Jesus' discourse on the Bread of Life, John 6:54-57: *"Except you eat of the flesh of the Son of man, and drink his blood, you shall not have life in you. He that eateth my flesh and drinketh my blood, hath life everlasting; and I will raise him up on the last day."* After emphasizing this repeatedly, some of Jesus' disciples found the words, "we must eat His Flesh and Blood," too hard to believe and they walked away, as seen in John 6:66 of the King James Bible: *From that time on many of his disciples went back, and walked no more with him."*

privacy of their chamber and the groom unveiled the inner sanctuary of His bride[128].

Dear brothers and sisters in Christ Jesus, the preaching of the Gospel of the Glory of Christ—the Gospel of the Holy Ghost—unveils the inner sanctuary of the Church/God's Bride in that it brings about the rising of God's mystical Kingdom. This rising penetrates, as in rents, the Church's inner veil, setting off the "apocalyptic events"—the blood shedding prophesied in the Book of Apocalypse/Revelation. This blood shedding of the last time saints is the seed which conceives new life, giving birth to the salt of the earth—God's children of Light. The Father's Name is hallowed—His King-dome comes and His Divine Will is done on earth as it is in Heaven. Halleluiah!

---

128 The beauty of the sacred mystery contained in the human body was captured in Saint John Paul II's talks on the Theology of the Body and so eloquently elaborated on in Christopher West's presentations on the Theology of the Body.

CHAPTER 12

"Come Holy Spirit, Come,
By means of the Powerful Intercession of
The Immaculate Heart of Mary
Thy well Beloved Spouse!"

The Great Consummation of Christ's Marriage to His Church

§

IN ORDER FOR THE GREAT Consummation of Christ's Marriage to His Bride, the Church, to take place the following knowledge must be implemented, proclaimed, and preached by the Church throughout the universal world.

1. The understanding that the Gospel of Christ's Glory necessitates the teaching that Jesus' risen and glorified Flesh, dispensed to us through the seven sacraments, is comprised of His Father's Sea of life giving Water and sanctifying Salt—as well as His Virgin Mother's purest and finest golden Olive Oil.

   Correspondingly, the Salt of the New Covenant must be properly restored to the Sacramental Rite of Baptism, to impress upon us our need to be set free from corruption—because nothing impure can unite with God.

2. Once the Bride, set free from corruption, unites in Sacred Unity/Divine Oneness with her beloved Spouse, she, like all brides, must call out, with heartfelt love and affection His Holy and Blessed Name: "Come Holy Spirit, come, by means of the powerful intercession of the Immaculate Heart of

Mary thy well beloved spouse."[129] This beseeching brings the Bride (the Church) into the most intimate relationship she (we) can have with her Bridegroom—the Consummation of their (our) Marriage.

This Great Consummation showers the Bride with a massive outpouring of the substance of God's Glory—His life giving Water, sanctifying Salt, and Virgin Olive Oil! This enormous profusion of God's Glory conceives and gives birth to God's children of light.

Through the following two keys Jesus gave to Peter, which have been passed down the ages through the chain of pontiffs for the past 2000 years, the Holy Spirit has been working through the <u>Proper Matter</u> and the <u>Proper Form</u> of the Catholic Church to build up the Body of Christ. The construction has been taking place through, with, and in the seven sacraments. Nevertheless, to bring the Church into completion and perfection, without wrinkle, spot or blemish, the full knowledge and understanding of these two keys had to be revealed and made known as it now is.

FIRST KEY

The Proper Matter consisting of:

<u>The proper material</u>: God's Life Giving Water, Sanctifying Salt, and Virgin Olive Oil. These are the elements of God's

---

129 In the Book of Psalms, also known as the P<u>salter</u>, David a hundred three times invokes praise, honor and glory to the Lord's Name. One example follows: *"Bring to the Lord glory and honour; bring to the Lord glory to His Name: adore ye the Lord in His holy court."* (Psalm 28:2, in the Douay-Rheims Bible)

risen Glory dispensed to us through the Precious Body and Blood of Jesus Christ in the seven sacraments.

The proper action: the Sign of the Cross—the cross of Jesus Christ/Christ Jesus!

The proper matter, consisting of the proper material and action, has existed since the time of Christ. These have been dispensed to us "most fully" by the true and faithful priests of all of the legitimate Rites within the Catholic Church.

Second Key

The Proper Form consisting of:

The proper words: In the Unity of the Holy Spirit.

The proper interior disposition: The proper words must be pronounced with the soul allowing the Divine Will of the Father to reign within, by the power of the Holy Spirit.

Through the understanding and proper interior disposition in the knowledge of God's blessed and holy Name of Unity—the Holy Spirit—our Heavenly Father's Name is hallowed, crowned with Glory, His Kingdom comes and His Will is done on earth as it is in Heaven.

(Recall the prefix "hal" in the word hallowed means salt and/ or more at salt. This is yet another confirmation that salt must be restored to the sacramental rite to bring about the "halo"—as in "Crowning" of Abba Father King of Glory. A halo, as you know, is a crown of light!)

The primary purpose of Jesus' mission on earth was, and is, to glorify His Father's Name—not His Name—but His Father's Name! As mighty, wonderful and powerful as Jesus' Name is, Jesus taught us to pray *"Our Father who art in heaven 'Hallowed be Thy Name"*[130] *thy Kingdom come."* Noting again how the words "hallowed be thy Name" precede the words "thy Kingdom Come." This stipulates that God's name "Father" must first, in the love, substance, oneness and unity of the Holy Spirit, be hallowed before His Kingdom can come. This powerful hallowing crowns Our Father with all the praise, honor and glory He is so deserving of!

Dear sisters and brothers, our Heavenly Father is delighted, like all fathers, when His children joining in peace, unity and oneness call out to Him with love, devotion and affection "Father!"

The Catechism of the Catholic Church teaches, "God revealed Himself to His people Israel by making His Name known to them. A name expresses a person's essence, identity and the meaning of this person's life. God has a Name: He is not an anonymous force. To disclose one's name is to make oneself known to others; in a way it is to hand oneself over by becoming accessible, capable of being known more intimately and addressed personally" (section 203).

The most accessible, intimate and personal name God revealed Himself to us under in the Old Covenant is Father. As seen in Isaiah 64:8: *"And now, O Lord, thou art Our Father, and we are clay and thou art our maker, and we all are the works of thy hands."*

Therefore, as the Father's obedient, loving and faithful children, our mission, like Jesus', must be to hallow our heavenly Father's name! Incidentally, calling our Father in Heaven "Abba" is a more personal term of endearment – like the word Daddy or Papa. This is seen in Romans 8:15-16, *"For you have not received the spirit of bondage*

---

130 At the consecration of the Holy Sacrifice of the Mass in the Roman Rite the people pray: "May the Lord accept the sacrifice at your hands for the praise and glory of His Name for our good and the good of all His holy Church."

again in fear; but you have received the spirit of adoption of sons whereby we cry: Abba [Father]. For the Spirit himself giveth testimony to our spirit that we are sons of God."

The Catechism then goes on to teach that God reveals Himself to us "Progressively under different Names" (Section 204). This speaks volumes because the last name God revealed Himself to us under—the Holy Ghost—would not only reveal to us the most complete picture of Him, but would be the New Name through which we would come into the most accessible, personal and intimate relationship we could possibly have with Him. This, of course, would be the Consummation of our Marriage![131]

The power in the all encompassing unity that defines this Sacred Name is expressed at the culmination of every Mass, the Great Doxology, when the priest holds up the Precious Body and Blood of Jesus Christ and proclaims: "Through Him, and with Him, and in Him, O God, almighty Father, in the Unity of the Holy Spirit, all glory and honor is yours, for ever and ever. Amen."

The power in God's New Name is reflected in the following Sacred Scripture: *"He that shall overcome, I will make him a pillar in the temple of my God; and he shall go out no more; and I will write upon him the name of my God, and the name of the city of my God, THE*

---

131 The Consummation: Envision a rising dome of salt within the earth – this is an analogy for the mystical Dome of Salt that is rising in our souls – this salt dome is about to have a breakthrough and give birth to the manifestation/revelation of the sons of God. The embrace of this knowledge brings about the martyrdom of the last time saints (the consummation of a marriage sheds blood), which is symbolized by the blood-red sunset that illumines the sky before the Dawn of the New Day. In this day (our 1000 year honeymoon) night shall be no more – Glory, Glory Hallelujah! (A thousand years in our time is equal to a day in the Lord, as seen in 2Peter 3:8. Thus, the thousand year period of peace would equate to the day of rest St. Paul in Hebrews chapter 4 is referring to when he writes: *There remaineth therefore a day of rest for the people of God. For he that hath entered into His rest, the same also hath rested from his works, as God did from his.* It is recommended the whole chapter be read.)

NEW JERUSALEM, which cometh down out of heaven, and MY NEW NAME." (Revelation 3:12)

Once again, when God's New Name, the last name He has revealed Himself to us under is invoked by the Church with all the heartfelt love, praise, honor, and exaltation it is so deserving of, God's Bride, the Church will enter into complete and perfect "oneness" with Him and all the amazing attributes of His Glory, *"For both he that sanctifieth, and they who are sanctified, are all one."* (Hebrews 2:11)

This Oneness of Sacred Unity, which involves a rising, brings about a massive explosion of God's Glory—the Great Consummation! This explosion of Glory unveils the New Jerusalem in our midst. The Father's Kingdom comes and His Will is done on earth as it is in Heaven. We will then have entered into the midst of God's Sea of Glory. The words of Our Lady of All Nations will have come to be realized: "The Holy Spirit of Peace will come if you pray, He is the Salt, He is the Water, He is the Light!"

His Light is His burning Love from which springs forth our glorified new Life. The life being the salt of the earth—His children of peace!

Of God's Holy, Blessed, and Glorious New Name, the Holy Ghost, Isaiah speaks: *"We have patiently waited for thee: Thy Name, and thy remembrance are the desire of the soul"* (Isaiah 26:8); Daniel 3:50 writes, *"And blessed is the Holy Name of thy 'Glory', and worthy to be praised, and exalted above all in all ages";* and as a final example David in Psalms 28:9/29:9 writes: *"And all in His Temple will speak of His Glory."*

The full knowledge of the Son of God now being revealed through St. Paul's Gospel of the Glory of Christ, is one and the same as the Gospel of the Holy Ghost, the Gospel of Truth and also the Eternal Gospel the angel of Revelation 14:6 is seen flying through the midst of Heaven with. The preaching of the Eternal

Gospel *"unto them that sitteth upon the earth, and over every nation, and tribe, and tongue and people"* is the Light that will bring about the New Dawn, the age when all Glory is given to the Father, all Glory is given to the Son, and all Glory is given to the Holy Spirit—as it was in the beginning, is now, and ever shall be, world without end. Amen.

Addendum

MORE INTERESTING FACTS ABOUT SALT: The salt of the earth comes to us in four different ways: from the ocean which is approximately 3% salt; from ocean brines which are approximately 15% salt; from the evaporation of sea basins which have created natural deposits mixed with impurities; and, from "salt domes" within the earth, relics of Noah's Flood.[132]

The following is a little history on salt domes: Salt domes are huge vertical cylinders of rock salt in the earth, usually a mile in diameter or larger. For example, the Avery Island rock salt dome, 140 miles west of New Orleans, sits atop one of America's largest salt domes from which two to three million tons of salt are quarried out every year—just scratching the surface. The television documentary <u>Salt Mines Our Modern Marvels</u> states that the Avery Salt Dome is literally larger than Mt. Everest. Ironically the commentator of this documentary continues: "Adding to the ghostly underground atmosphere is salt, lots of it—surprisingly beautiful—glistening everywhere. There are six levels to this labyrinth the deepest 1500 feet down, more than 100 miles of roads, caverns and work stations that glow with unexpected color."

---

132 John Morris, <u>Does Salt Come From Evaporated Sea Water</u>? http://www.icr.org/article/532/

This documentary also states that salt beds can stretch horizontally for hundreds of miles—one of the largest extending all the way from upstate New York, beneath Lake Erie, to western Michigan. Salt domes and salt beds are found throughout the world, i.e. in the Unites States, Canada, Nova Scotia, South America, China, Russia, Germany, Hungary, and Romania.

Another interesting rock salt dome that the documentary points out happens to be under a village in central Poland, the homeland of Saint John Paul II. The documentary states that: "this salt mine has been in operation for over seven centuries and is comprised of nine levels, 240,000 chambers, 125 miles of tunnels, ranging from 200 to 1100 feet underground. Of peak interest is the fact that one of Poland's oldest and most beautiful chapels is carved in this mine out of "pure rock salt." It took 67 years to complete this beautiful chapel whose chandeliers, icons, crucifix of Christ, altar—everything—is carved entirely out of pure rock salt. The chapel as well as the strange pools and lakes have attracted tourists since the 17th century which explains why the United Nations has placed "Wieliczka (Krakow)" on its World Heritage list as one of the cultural treasures of mankind. This informative documentary ends quite prophetically: "Salt, the ultimate preservative, has safeguarded our health, our food, our gold, and now quite possibly our future. A future that will no doubt contrive new uses for this most humble and versatile mineral!"

Lightning and Thunder: The Science Daily News Release of November 11, 03 was entitled "Thunderstorm Research Shocks Conventional Theories; Florida Tech Physicist Throws Open Debate on Lightning's Cause." The article begins, "If Joseph Dwyer, Florida Tech associate professor of physics, is right, then a lot of what we thought we knew about thunderstorms and lightning is probably wrong." The article ends, "Although everyone is familiar with lightning, we still don't know much about how it really works.' Said Dwyer."

The comment I would have liked to pose at this open debate is that since lightning is electric and the most common nuclei of a cloud is salt, which is an electrolyte, would not the cloud's salt nuclei—coupled with the right weather conditions—be responsible for sparking lightning?

In addition, since "heat lightning" throws off many colors of the white light spectrum, then would it not be reasonable to surmise that the cloud's salt nuclei would be responsible for these colors. After all, these beautiful colors could not project from a cloud whose nuclei consist of dust or air pollutants. These colors which bring to mind the beautiful unexpected colors of the salt mines!

An interesting theory that has to do with salt and lightning follows: I remember reading that the brilliant streak of lightning is due to the metal sodium. This proves fascinating when you consider that salt is made up of the two elements sodium and chloride and that when you put salt in water these two elements, sodium (+) and chloride (-), **disassociate** into electrically charged particles.

What's fascinating about this is that Lucifer, whose name means light bearer, was at one time one with God's Light – God whose Light, as we have seen, is mystically comprised of salt and water. In fact, Lucifer was the brightest of God's angels—until his pride, envy, and jealousy caused him to sin against God and the Woman.

So, if you think about it, since nothing impure can exist in Heaven, this means that when Lucifer sinned, God had to "disassociate" him from His Light. Then in order for this disassociation to take place God's atomic substance salt would have had to split—as in disassociate into two parts: one expelling Lucifer with God's Light (lighting—sodium +), the other part sounding off thunder (chloride -).

Note how this explains Luke 10:18: "*I saw Satan [Lucifer] falling from heaven like LIGHTNING.*" [133]

When it comes to lightning and thunder first you see the lightning; next there is the eerie silence; and then comes the "rumbling thunder." The silence that takes place in between the lightning and thunder would explain the silence in Chapter 8 of the Book of Revelation where we learn that when the "seventh seal is opened" "*there was 'silence' in Heaven, as it were for half an hour.*" (8:1) The chapter follows this up saying that there were "*thunders and voices and lightnings, and a great earthquake.*'" (Recollect that the great earthquake is also activated by salt—the rising rock salt domes hidden within the earth. *For everyone shall be salted with salt!* Mark 9:48)

Although scientists admit that lightning and thunder is a very complicated subject that is not fully understood, they do agree that the electrical discharge in lighting causes a sudden expansion of air. This expansion of air corresponds with an immense and most brilliant electrical discharge in lightning (symbolized by the great spiritual enlightenment of the Gospel of the Glory of Christ) that will cast Lucifer and his evil cohorts into the abyss of hell for a period of 1000 years. This removal of evil renders all things silent for *half an hour.* Ah... the power of silence!

Salt: A Three-Dimensional, White, Crystalline, Perfectly Cube-Shaped, Immutable Substance: In continuing to explore the theory that salt represents the substance of God's Glory, the author was amazed by the knowledge that began to unfold as she increased her knowledge of this humble, pure, and simple substance.

---

133 Here are two other scripture verses on God's light to give thought to: *For as the 'lightning' that lightened up under heaven, shineth unto the parts that are under haven, so shall the Son of Man be in His day.* (Luke 17:24) *And then the wicked one shall be revealed whom the Lord Jesus shall kill with the spirit of His mouth; and shall destroy with the 'brightness of His coming.'* (2 Thessalonians 2:8)

For example, salt is a three-dimensional, white, crystalline, perfectly cube-shaped, immutable substance. Note how these characteristics mirror the mystery of the Most Holy Trinity:

- The "three" dimensions correspond to the revelation in time of the three Divine Persons of the Most Blessed Trinity—the three measures of meal!
- The white crystalline color corresponds to the description of Jesus' [134]glorified body as depicted in the Bible and also by visionaries.
- The cube shape corresponds to the New Jerusalem whose walls are measured a hundred and forty-four cubits.[135]
- The immutability of salt in its solid state represents God who is unchanging—He is the same yesterday, today and always.

"The Glory of God appeared in a Cloud" Exodus 16:10:" The following are passages of Sacred Scripture the author came across while perusing the Bible to confirm her reflection on the link between God's Glory and Water and Salt.

> *"Nor could the priests stand and minister by reason of the 'cloud.' For the 'glory' of the Lord had filled the house of God."* (II Paralipomenon/Chronicles 5:14).

"Give ye 'Glory' to God for Israel, His magnificence and power is in the 'clouds." (Psalm 67:35)

---

134 In St. Matthew's account of Jesus' transfiguration it is written: *And He was transfigured before them. And His face did shine as the sun: and His garments became white as snow.* (Matthew 17:2)

135 Of the New Jerusalem it is written in the Book of Revelation 21:16-17: *And the city lieth in a foursquare... And he measured the wall thereof a hundred forty-four 'cubits' the 'measure of a man, which is an angel.'* Bringing to mind Jesus Christ in whom the fullness of all things, the three measures of meal, dwells.

"And then they shall see these things, and the Majesty of the Lord shall appear, and there shall be a 'cloud' as it was also showed to Moses..." (II Machabees 2:8)

"And then shall appear the "sign of the Son of Man in Heaven," and then shall all tribes of the earth mourn: and they shall see the Son of Man coming in the 'cloud' of Heaven with much power and majesty." (Matthew 24:30)

"Who is the father of the rain? Or who 'begot' the drops of dew? Out of whose 'womb' came the ice, and the frost from Heaven who that 'gendered it." (Job 38:28-29)

I had also thought about the Israelites who were sustained for 40 years in the desert on manna. Manna, which the Bible says was "dew" from heaven. Dew being a cloud come down from Heaven!

Then I recalled the words of the prophet Isaiah 60:1-8, who called God's *Glory* the *mist* on His people. Isaias also talks about: *"when the multitude of the 'sea' shall be converted,"* and he goes on to say: *"who are these that fly as 'clouds', and as doves to their windows?"*

I was also given over to reflect on Ecclesiasticus (Sirach) 43:24: *"A present remedy for all is the speedy coming of a 'cloud' and the 'dew' that meeteth it."* The cloud represents the Messiah's coming in Glory; the dew represents His Glory – Salt and Water – which we receive through the Seven Sacraments.

And wasn't it dew from Heaven that saved Sidrach, Misach, and Abdenago from burning in the flaming furnace of fire? They, being *"bathed in dew from heaven"* danced in the midst of flames glorifying and praising God with the beautiful canticle of creation—see Daniel 3:20-26 and 50-90.

Could it have been a coincidence that the author had been reading the The Life of Jesus Christ by Blessed Anne Catherine Emmerick, in which she writes about Abraham's reception of the Old Covenant Sacrament as follows: "Then with both hands the angel held something like a little luminous Cloud toward Abraham's breast. I saw it entering him, and I felt as if he was receiving the Blessed Sacrament." (Vol. 1, page 85)

It seemed to make sense that if God's Glory is symbolized by the water and salt from the Cloud of His Glory and we are to share in His Glory—then our lives, as well, would depend on water and salt—as was just depicted by His prophets. This really isn't so hard to fathom when you consider that the two most vital components of our earthly existence are water and salt.

These very elements presented by scripture as the beginning and the first elements, are the images of God we are made in. These are the elements St. Paul said must be taught again—the elements that God, in the Book of Isaiah, said He would declare before they were about to "spring forth." He is now declaring them because they are about to spring forth—into what Saint John Paul II has prophesied as the "New Spring Time."

**WHEN YOU THINK ABOUT IT,
WE HAVE BEEN LIKE FISH
IN THE OCEAN
LOOKING FOR WATER!**

Made in the USA
Columbia, SC
28 March 2018